Mental Illness

"The Mystery of Mysteries That Will Never Be Solved"

Or is it?

Welcome to the world of Epistemic Psychology and the origins of Mental Illness

By
Patricia Lear

Disclaimer

Before you read on

This book was written to teach the readers how the Mind works so they can better understand their own mental illness. It teaches about healing the nonphysical Mind through understanding how Mind and Thought works. Physical medicine is often used by those with mental problems which is why there is a need for this disclaimer though this book only teaches how the Mind operates and how that operation relates to mental disorders and returning the Mind to its natural healthy state of being.

The information in this book is true and complete to the best of my knowledge.

By continuing to read this book you are acknowledging the following:

1) The views and opinions expressed here are not to be taken as medical advice. 2) The information provided in this book is for educational purposes and does not substitute for professional medical advice or treatment. 3)The author is not liable for anything associated with using or acting upon the information in this book. 4)The writer of this book shall not be liable for any indirect, incidental, special, consequential or punitive damages or loss of profits or revenues whether incurred directly or indirectly from the use of the information in this book. 5) This book contains information relating to mental epistemology for self-care and is not intended to replace medical advice. 6) The publisher and author disclaim any liability for any outcomes that may occur from applying what is suggested in this book. 7) Any decision concerning your mental or physical health care is between you and your doctor. 8) The act of continuing to read this book and your use of the information therein constitutes a legally binding agreement that you acknowledge and take responsibility for your use of the information herein.

These are the rules for continuing to use this book.

As of the writing of this book, mental illnesses have been dealt with either through teaching the person how to cope with the illness and/or taking drugs. Mental illnesses are considered to be unable to be cured. Mostly that is because they are in no way understood…

until now

It is my hope that this book will teach you how to heal your own mental illness or assist in the healing of others and bring blessings to all who read it.

Welcome to the world of Epistemic Psychology

Table of Contents

People go to psychiatrists in a desperate attempt to be healed. Sometimes they do so because they are about to do something that is life destroying and they are hoping to stop what they are about to do. Often, they leave angry and the next thing the psychiatrist knows is that the person's life and possibly the life of someone they hurt is over.

Those who are in Psychiatry for the right reasons want to help the people who come to them and they try with all they know but, in many instances, they simply cannot solve the problem.

Some people refer to the first disorder I discovered as the "Mystery of Mysteries" that will never be solved.

But what if it isn't?

I was a special education teacher probably from the day I was born. That seems like a zillion years ago. I once took a test on the Internet on what career I should choose. I left out all things concerning teaching and pressed the button. The word teacher came up in big letters. I was doomed.

I have had certificates to teach in three states and in multiple subjects, special education and specialized education. I had a degree in human relations and child development. I had all the bells and whistles.

Though I didn't want a degree in psychology, I studied people therefore studied psychology from superficial disorders like envy to the most bizarre like the people who believe they have too many legs and try to cut one off. By the way, the doctors brilliantly heal that situation by putting the patient in the hospital to remove a leg, giving the patient three cards, two that say keep and one that says remove and leaving the patient to figure out how to put three cards on two legs.

I have understood and have been dedicated to special people all of my life. Sometimes they would follow me places. My first student was when I was nine. His name was David. Then there was Joan. Then there was James all while I was in elementary school.

But never in my life did I think I would understand mental illness and what it truly is.

Never in my life did I think I would know the physical cause of mental illness.

Never in my life did I think I would be writing about the unknown situation that caused mental illness.

And never in my life did I think I would have discovered the answer to "The Mystery of Mysteries that will Never Be Solved". Never in my life did I think I would be writing a book on it and other related disorders. Never in my life did I think I would have the answers psychiatrists could not figure out.

Though I would study the behaviors of people in general and the writings of researchers my main focus was special education children or better said children with developmental disabilities.

In the beginning, I assumed that all developmental disabilities were related to intellectual impairment of one sort or another and a person with normal intelligence would have problems that fell within the field of Psychology meaning relating to things that were caused by living life and certainly not in another field altogether.

It would be decades from the time the first subject crossed my path that I would realize that a person could have a genius IQ and a developmental disability at the same time, that most mental illnesses are really disorders that began before birth and what the problem really is.

I did not realize that a person could have a disability or multiple disabilities that began before birth just as those with developmental disabilities yet their intellect remained intact. It simply did not dawn on me.

When I realized what was going on, it was in the worst of circumstances with horrible crime and death resulting from the behavior of the subject that had crossed my path. I had to learn more. I had to find others. And I surely did.

The number of men, women, boys, girls who had virtually the same criminal disorder, the same basic symptoms, and were on the same path toward devastation was astounding. The number who had high or genus IQ levels and why was just as shocking.

Just one revelation began my journey toward understanding the Mind, the Thought components in the Mind, what I call the "Natural State of Being" and what happened to make things go so terribly wrong.

I hope I am able to convey what I have learned and lead you into the understanding that can bring healing to those who are currently told about their situation, "There is no cure."

This book contains repetitive stories and explanations but it contains no fluff. In order to understand this very complex information you will need to not read what is here but read it and contemplate what is being taught. Apply it to life and mental disorders and you will see the whole picture. Remember, the causes of mental illnesses have eluded humanity for a very long time. Only contemplation and work will give you the answers to what mental illness really is.

I
The Psychologies

CHAPTER 1
Common Psychology

"All truths are easy to understand once they are discovered. The point is discovering them" – Galileo

My aunt had diabetes. As a young girl of ten I would visit her every few months. Each time I saw her there was another part removed. First it was her foot, then her leg then the other leg and so on. I remember thinking, as a child would, that next time I see her only her head would be on the wheelchair.

At that time, decades ago, they were looking at what caused her limbs to become gangrenous never thinking it would be something in the blood having to do with the pancreatic gland near the stomach. The concept was too far away from what would seem to be the problem.

Today that cure that was unconnected to the physical limbs of the body is well known, understood and accepted.

It is my hope you will contemplate and understand the answers presented here about mental illness as the world has understood and accepted the situation concerning diabetes.

The Psychologies are evolving.

Contrary to the belief by most that Psychology and psychoanalysis have been around since the dawn of time, they actually began slowly in the 1800s. The year 1874 marked the official start of psychology as a scientific discipline or better said as a realization that the problem was mental and thought related.

In the 1800s Sigmund Freud introduced the concept that the unconscious mind and early childhood experiences caused behavioral issues a concept that was somewhat true but was by far not the whole story.

In the earlier years the belief was that women who were behaving "erratically" did so because they were reacting to damage felt when they realized they didn't have a penis, which Freud called "Penis Envy". There was also the belief that women's behavior was due to uterine problems such as a roving or displaced uterus or a wondering womb that did not stay in one place and moved about the body causing the other organs to react. Since this too was believed to have caused behavioral issues in females the removal of the uterus or a hysterectomy was used as a curative procedure.

The term hysteria, a word derived from the Greek word hystera which means uterus, comes from this belief that the uterus was the cause of problems concerning females. They believed that "there was no ailment more dangerous for a woman than her womb spontaneously wandering around her abdominal cavity".

For some genital massage done by an approved provider was practiced as a solution to the unusual behavior. Some called a woman's desire to learn and go to college "a temporary nervous condition - a slight hysterical tendency". It was believed that marriage, intercourse and pregnancy would do the trick to remove that hysterical tendency and it proved true that marriage, and children certainly could inadvertently alleviate the thought of going to college.

Males for the most part, having no womb or uterus, were believed to be possessed by the devil and in need of an exorcism when their behavior could not be logically explained.

For both male and female the practice of Phrenology was considered the answer. The shape and size of the cranium and bumps on the skull were thought to explain mental issues. The Edinburgh Phrenological Society was formed in 1820. This belief was influential from 1810 to 1840.

The point is that the field of Psychology is still evolving. We are learning each day that we keep an open mind. New things are being learned and discovered all the time.

We have come a long way from believing that moving uteri and devils are causing behavioral problems but we still have a long way to go. We still have those who seek an answer and walk away without one. We still have people who are considered evil instead of sick and are seen as human monsters who were born evil. And knowing some of their behaviors one can understand that philosophy but that doesn't make it any less incorrect.

Today we have Psychology. Psychology is "the scientific study of the human mind and its functions especially those affecting behavior in a given context." Yet many mental illnesses cannot be explained through Psychology of today. Many people go to psychiatrists only to end up thinking they cannot be helped and many people go to psychiatrists before taking destructive actions. Some even study Psychology or Neurology to heal themselves to no avail.

So why is it that for so many Psychology does not work? Why are there still disorders of the mind that are simply left unexplained. Why does it state in the DSM-5, (the Diagnostic and Statistical Manual of Mental Disorders published by the American Psychiatric Association that serves as the principal authority of psychiatric disorders) concerning so many illnesses that "there is no cure"? Even when there is a "diagnosis" it is simply the placement of a label and number but not an explanation.

The reason that what we call Psychology today often does not work is that the field of Psychology is the study of the human mind after birth, the effects of life and living on a person and what the person thinks from their life experiences. There also is no understanding of the components that make the human mind and their influence on mental illness.

To rely only on the field of Psychology as we know it without understanding the whole picture would be to leave many unhealed of their mental illnesses. And that is what is currently happening.

So, why does psychology often not work?

Psychologies are evolving but the way the child was made is exactly the same as it was thousands of years ago.

Though there are many theories in the field of Psychology and types of Psychology like environmental psychology, evolutionary psychology, occupational psychology, social Psychology, Neuropsychology, I would say there is only one Psychology since Psychology is simply the study of the Mind or sometimes people think it is the study of the brain. The Psychologies mentioned overlap each other and are usually connected to an outside influence. Those in the psychology field may show the person with a disorder how to cope with a situation but few if any can tell you why a disorder happens, how it happens and how to cure it. Most merely teach how to cope and offer drugs. These fields of psychology deal with the person's reaction to the world in which they live and have lived since birth.

Developmental Psychology, and Cognitive Psychology are different. Cognitive psychology deals with how we think and helps understand the human brain which is the very problem. The brain does nothing. It is the Mind that needs to be understood. This thought that the problem is the brain leads cognitive psychologists in the wrong direction from the start. Developmental Psychology deals with how a person grows and develops over a lifetime.

The problem with cognitive and developmental psychologies is that both do not have a standard in which to evaluate what is going on. They have a behavioral norm. When that norm is not acted upon either because of a single activity or multiple activities called symptoms it could be said the person has a mental illness. That illness is then registered in the DSM and given a name and number.

Developmental Psychology and Cognitive Psychology can be good tools if they deal with the thoughts that are used for development and cognition and build upon those thoughts. It is the thought in the Mind that is important since the brain is merely a conduit to the body.

There are times when people simply need to tell another what is bothering them or get another opinion about a specific situation. There are times when a person simply needs to feel they are loved or cared about by someone. Psychology can help in this area as well.

A note on the DSM.

The funny, or maybe not so funny, thing is that the DSM changes all the time. The current DSM is called DSM5 because it has changed removing and adding mental illnesses 4 times prior. Yes, one minute a person is mentally ill because a book says so and the next the person is not mentally ill because a book says so.

In the DSM, there are axioms and categories and subcategories. But very few, if any, origins or causes or explanations. There are often no explanations for whatever the person is thinking to cause them to fit into a particular category. The book consists of lists and categories of lists and numbers but provides little or no real answers and claims to not be for therapeutic purposes.

Unbeknownst to psychiatrists many disorders in the DSM are really disorders that began in the unborn child. These disorders could include disorders that have the same symptoms as post birth disorders.

Often disorders that cause what is believed to be illogical behavior are given a label in the DSM and those with such disorders are usually considered inexplicably untreatable or unhealable. Those with criminal behavior may be labeled as well and are sometimes considered simply evil or not considered at all.

John Forbes Nash, Jr. attended Carnegie Institute of Technology where a professor said of him that "He is a mathematical genius." and though accepted at Harvard he went to Princeton University instead. He was an American mathematician who made fundamental contributions to game theory, real algebraic geometry, differential geometry, and partial differential equations. Nash was one of three men awarded the 1994 Nobel Memorial Prize in Economics and later awarded with another man the Abel Prize for his contribution to the field of partial differential equations among other awards. He was known for the Nash Equilibrium. His story was told in the movie A Beautiful Mind with Russell Crowe.

John Nash showed signs of "mental disturbances" in the early months of 1959 and later was diagnosed with severe schizophrenia. He described a process of change "from scientific rationality of thinking into the delusional thinking characteristic of persons who are psychiatrically diagnosed as 'schizophrenic' or 'paranoid schizophrenic".

"If you put three mental health clinicians in a room with one client, you'll get four different diagnoses." - John Nash

John Nash would know full well that three mental health clinicians and one client would give four diagnoses.

The question is when and why did he lose his footing as his high IQ led to the belief that he was basically a mentally normal person prior to his collapse. If my research is correct John Nash had a mental disorder from birth that led to his unusual behavior prior to his becoming schizophrenic.

It also led to his high IQ which I will explain later. Had he not been told that his work was incorrect he may have simply stayed a bit weird. John Nash's instability was from a loss that happened before birth, which you will learn about. This loss that made him different also made him very smart and does so for many who suffer a loss before birth. Later when his world of math collapsed or seemed to collapse the instability from the before birth disorder caused him to be unable to adequately handle the situation and he was diagnosed schizophrenic. The schizophrenia was a post birth reaction to what was a before birth disorder. This is not uncommon.

Another example of the difference between psychiatric disorders and disorders caused by what happened in the unborn baby is the story of Sybil. Her story was made into a movie starring Sally Field called <u>Sybil</u>. Sybil was diagnosed later in her life with multiple personality disorder which could be called a mental disorder but the disorder did not occur before birth. Her disorder was due to severe abuse during her lifetime. It is important to make this distinction in order to figure out what the thought is that needs to be corrected or needs to be placed.

From here on the word Mind and the word Thought will be capitalized as they are important words. The Thoughts that are acquired after the child is born will be called Life Acquired Thoughts and Thoughts planted before birth will be called Prebirth Thoughts. This is for separation when explaining the various mental illness disorders.

CHAPTER 2
Epistemic Psychology

Psychology is defined as "the scientific study of the human mind and its functions especially those affecting behavior in a given context." The word epistemic is related to the word epistemology which means the study of the nature and grounds of knowledge. Epistemic Psychology is the study the human psyche through understanding the components of the Mind and components of Thoughts.

This is a field of study of the world of Mind and the Thoughts that are placed before birth. Though it may not be considered "scientific" by physical standards it proves itself to be real and true since Mind in itself is not physical and post birth psychology does not answer the question of causation of many mental disorders nor does it present any means of healing.

The body is the set of cells that work in unison. Grey's Anatomy is a book that details how that set of cells called the body works. It tells about blood pressure, hormones, what its numbers should be and so on. But it refers only to the physical body.

The world of Psychiatry typically deals with situations that come from living in the world. And, of course, books on Psychiatry deal with situations that come from living in the world.

This book can be considered the Grey's Anatomy of the Mind. Maybe it would be better said this book is the Grey's Anatomy of what makes up the Mind, how it is constructed, the building blocks of Thoughts that make up the Mind, the Thoughts that work in unison, the Thoughts that work alone, the Thoughts placed in the being before it is born for use throughout its life. In other words, the whole gestalt of Mind.

Understanding the Mind completely would take decoding hundreds of thousands of individual thoughts which is what this book will do when completed. The number of cells in the body is enormous and they are part of a system that is complex and intricate. The number of thoughts in the Mind of the unborn baby is enormous as well and they are part of a system that is complex and intricate.

Just like in the body where there are cells that work in unison with other cells that make up what we call an organ, there are Thoughts that are connected to other thoughts that work in unison as well. The plan these Thoughts use is called Schema by Psychologist Jean Piaget. There are also

Thoughts that are on timers to be activated later. There are Thoughts that are placed in the Mind before birth that deactivate and are replaced with other Thoughts. There are Thoughts that simply stop being active. There are Thoughts that are more active than others. There are Thoughts that are unconscious. There are Thoughts that are a bit buried. And there are Thoughts that are placed in memory.

All of these Thoughts are already in the baby when it leaves the birth canal if nothing interferes with their placement and they are set to work immediately though some may be activated later.

The placement of these Thoughts in the Mind of the unborn baby begins somewhere very close to or upon conception and ends before the 20th week of gestation since at that point if the baby is born it is able to grow naturally without incident in its life. These Thoughts, of course, are placed in the Mind of the unborn baby prior to the formation of purposely retrievable memory.

This "Other" Psychology Psychologists typically never use

It needs to be stated that Memory in the new born baby and for a long time after birth is used to grow the Mind to use with the body and what is learned is retrievable for that purpose. Early memories are at first not at all consciously retrievable but later become sporadically consciously retrievable. Some memories never become consciously retrievable like the memories of how to learn.

Early on even if a memory is consciously retrievable what is remembered is not necessarily consciously understood. It all takes time as one by one the Thoughts placed before birth and ones learned afterward are used by the child and placed in memory.

If something goes wrong with Thoughts that should have been planted in the early life of the child and there is no prior memory of the Thoughts for comparison the child will be unable to heal itself. This would be because they have no ability to remember when they had the Thought.

At times it is difficult to tell whether what is causing certain behaviors is due to what happened before birth or after birth in some of the disorders in this book.

It is very hard for an outside person to heal another in the field of Psychiatry because we are so complex. This book offers the reader the opportunity and knowledge for self-healing as long as the person has the cognition to do so.

II
The Perfect Mind

CHAPTER 3
The Natural State of Being/The First Revelation

Now that you know there are two kinds of Psychiatry, one that deals with Thoughts acquired after birth and the other that deals with Thoughts before birth, and that since both consider themselves to be studies of the "human mind" one needs to define the "human mind" and understand what the "human mind" actually is.

Greys Anatomy is a book that details how the physical body works including the brain since the brain, which is simply a conduit to the body, is physical. But the brain and the body are nothing without the Mind. And the Mind is made of Thoughts. Therefore, there needs to be a book that shows the intelligently constructed workings of the Mind and its component Thoughts.

This conglomeration of Thoughts each with their individual instructions and collective instructions form the Mind itself as a unit. Analyzing this Mind and its component Thoughts will allow me to explain how to heal mental illnesses. This is the goal of this mental Greys Anatomy book you are reading.

The Mind is a conglomeration of Thoughts that is purposely constructed as a singular unit. It is complete and perfect and is the mechanism that runs the body through the conduit that is the brain. This conglomeration of Thoughts is exactly the same for every human just as the body is the same for each human except for the added Thoughts that account for traits, personality and talent.

The Mind as a conglomeration of Thoughts is made up of individual Thoughts that each have their own Thought instruction. They work individually and as a unit just as the cells of the body work individually with their individual instructions and also work as a singular organ.

Just as the body is not simply a place where organs are kept but work in unison, the Mind is not simply place where Thoughts and their instructions are kept and work in unison. The cells of the body are united to make up the body. The Thoughts in the Mind are united to make up the Mind. And they together make the person or the self.

The mental unit called the Mind that is perfect and works as it was planned to work that was placed before the baby was born is what I call "The Natural State of Being". It is what is supposed to be for everyone. It is what is naturally supposed to be. It is living perfection of the Mind.

The perfect Thoughts with their perfect instructions are placed in the Mind of the being long before it is born to be used throughout its life. This "natural state" is the way nature or God would make a person and it is perfect.

It is the understanding of this "Natural State of Being" that is missing in the field of Psychology and without that understanding healing anything that was caused before birth would be as difficult as trying to heal the body without Grey's Anatomy.

Making the perfect human being

Nothing can be done when the original design is flawed. There is no fixing what was made defective from the start. But humans are not made defective in any way. The plan is, was and always has been perfect...until something goes wrong in its application.

The discovery of the Natural State of Being and the Thought components that make up the Mind of the perfect human was brought about by a progression of events. What you read in this book took decades to uncover. It began over forty years ago.

The first step toward healing is understanding "The Natural State of Being", the basic program of Mind and its Thoughts.

Before I talk about the "Natural State of Being" that is put into place in the human after conception and long before birth., I have to properly convey to you something that is the basis of all things in this book. It has to be understood that "The Natural State of Being" had to have been meticulously planned. The building of the human being and the building of the Mind of the human being with so many integral and connecting parts, some of which you are going to learn about here, that were placed in the unborn baby could not have been random or a matter of happenstance.

Though I didn't want to say this because I didn't want to lose even one person especially if they need this information to survive but to me the fact that the Thoughts were placed and placed in the way they were means it had to be done by an intelligence meaning by God. That is my belief.

For me to explain the plan that was placed in the unborn child and what went wrong I have to rely on the plan itself which is "The Natural State of Being" and that plan has to be understood as being an actual detailed contemplated preconceived plan. And I believe someone had to make the plan. It's as simple as that.

A doctor cannot fix a body without knowing how a normal body functions. A doctor cannot know one has high blood pressure without knowing what normal blood pressure would be. Just the same one cannot fix a psyche without knowing how a normal psyche functions. Therefore, in both cases one has to know how the physical or mental being is made.

The material structure of the human is its physical anatomy which has been studied for a very long time and is fairly well documented in books like Grey's Anatomy.

The non-material or mental structure of the human has an anatomy as well. It is the natural structure or state of how human beings are non-materially or mentally made. It is preplanned and the same for all except for individual personality details, just as the plan for the body is preplanned except for individual personal physical details.

One of the most important things, if not the most important thing, needed to understand the Mind of the human and its disorders is "The Natural State of Being".

The "Natural State of Physical Being" is the basis of all things physically human. While, for the sake of this book, what I call "The Natural State of Being" refers to what is the basis of all things mentally human.

In this "Natural State of Being" lies the Concept Thoughts and the Action Thoughts that make all things human mentally happen and therefore, along with the body, physically happen.

This mental structure along with its drive in "The Natural State of Being" as you will learn, causes the action for all human physical tasks that come from the Mind to be performed. It, along with individual choice, is the cause in humans of wonder and beauty or discord and damage.

Since one of the most important things that I could teach you is about the non-material preplanned mental structure that is placed in every human before birth which I call their "Natural State of Being" I am going to try to explain "The Natural State of Being" using the analogy of the cells of the body.

I am going to take you through the process so congratulations we are going to make a baby. Sorry, it will not be done the typical fun way. We are going to make a baby the way God or nature would have done it from scratch.

The plan for the physical cells of the body to do what they need to do is predetermined and fixed as most people know. Everyone in their perfect physical state has a "Natural State of (physical) Being" of one head, two arms, one torso, two legs, ten fingers, one heart and so on.

The plan for the cells of the body is fixed for everyone barring something going wrong except for personal traits like your father's nose or Aunt Mimi's feet.

I want to start at the very, very beginning to explain to you what happened materially and nonmaterially to produce a human being with all its body parts and cognition.

Bear with me, there is a point to this way of explaining what happened.

Physically:

If we start physically from the very beginning, we have the naturally planned sequence of the sperm swimming through the cervix and the fallopian tubes toward the egg by use if its long tail. As it gets closer to the egg the planned sequence is that the head of the sperm hardens to force entry into the egg. The sperm meets the egg and enters causing the next part of the sequence to be that the egg closes up so that the other billion or so sperms are not able to enter so the mother does not give birth to a billion babies at once.

Thank goodness for that plan!

Once fertilized the egg splits and splits. But the cells do not simply reproduce haphazardly just for the purpose of making more and more cells. There is a set plan for each one of the cells to become a cellular piece of a particular larger organ like a lung or a heart and so on. If there was not a set plan, we would simply be a blob of cells laying on the floor.

So why am I telling you this? Because you need to see the importance of the overall preset plan that is "The Natural State of (physical) Being" and how the mental plan is a bit different.

Mentally:

You probably have no problem understanding and believing that there is a preset plan in the physical building and development of the basic human being since you can see it happening. The plan of two legs, one head, one torso, two arms and so on is a plan that is set and waiting to be put in place upon conception. Preplanned Thoughts are placed in each of the cells giving them instructions to split and split but to do so in sequence with each to simultaneously become what they were programmed or planned to be. Therefore, the cells are splitting and the parts of the body are growing simultaneously into their finished parts.

The cognitive plan is a bit different. The physical plan is set with the cells being already instructed through preplaced Thoughts as to what they are to do and they do so simultaneously as they build into the particular organs they are to become. The mental plan, however, is one where Thoughts are placed in the Mind of the being one after another as it grows within the womb. These Thoughts can be individual or part of a sequence or part of a set. This is a big difference.

The first moment of conception is the first time the preplanned physical plan and the preplanned mental plan are put into play for that human. The physical plan is placed at once in the human being and grows as each cell does what it was already programmed to do.

From the first moment of conception to birth, and, of course after, the preset plan for physical development of the human being is placed and starts and continues as it is programmed to do with the program already in place in each cell from the beginning.

For mental development in the human being the unborn child does NOT have the set program already planted in its Mind. Though the plan is already made, each Thought is not planted at once in the being at conception as it is in the physical plan. This implantation beginning from conception or close to it is gradual with different individual Thoughts or Thought sequences being planted as time goes on and the unborn (not yet called a baby) baby grows.

This difference between how the physical part of the human is built with cells all going their separate ways and how the mental part of the human is built is a very important part in understanding "The Natural State of Being" of the Mind and the disorders that happen when the Thoughts that should be placed in "The Natural State of Being" of the Mind are not placed.

In number, Thoughts that make up the Mind are like the cells of the body. There are probably hundreds of thousands if not millions or billions and they work in unison as the cells of the body work in unison.

Here I have put in some Thoughts that are in the Prebirth Mind that are for immediate use upon birth or activated later. They will give you an idea of how intricate the Thoughts are and what it takes to make up the human Mind. They were taken from the work of Jean Piaget. The Thought or Thoughts to learn. The Thought that they have a physical body. The Thought of being able to turn off Thoughts. The Thought of the self as a whole. The Thought to know one's place in the world. The Thought to imagine. The Thought to know reality from unreality? The Thought to choose right from wrong. The Thought to be happy. The Thought that we are seen by others. The Thought that we live in a stable world. The Thought of the concepts of being a child, a teenager, an adult. The Thought of being separate from others. The thought of being separate from the surrounding world. The Thought of things being right. The Thought that objects are permanent. The Thought that there are objects that can't go through other objects. The Thought that we should not be afraid. The Thought that we can recall. The Thought that there is an order to things. The Thought that your Mind is connected to your body. And of course, there are so many more. Thank you. Mr. Piaget.

Note: Owning the book of Grey's Anatomy does not make one a doctor. The person has to understand it and more than that the person has to use it. Using Grey's Anatomy by a doctor to heal the physical body is the same as using "The Natural State of Being" of the Mind to heal mental illnesses. Also, this book is a work in progress. It is far from showing all that needs to be learned but it is a start and it gives you the basics.

CHAPTER 4
General Thoughts of the Mind

PURPOSE OF THIS CHAPTER: To teach of Thoughts that are placed that apply to the entire Mind as a whole.

There are Thoughts in the Mind that oversee Thoughts in the Mind itself in general. These Thoughts are not specific to a particular task but relate to other Thoughts. These overall Thoughts are depth, speed, memory, equilibrium, the self. learning, holding a Thought while thinking another, Truth and Love.

Depth

Before you read this, I strongly urge you to watch the movie <u>Sybil</u> starring Sally Field. Sybil is the true story of a woman with multiple personalities and her journey toward healing. She lived through horrible situations and survived. But the reason for watching the movie is to understand the depth of the Mind.

The movie should be watched in the dark to get the full effect of what happened with Sybil and the deep dark journey into her psyche. This will give you an idea of what I am trying to convey here and how deep the despair could be.

The Mind is like a deep dark cave where the person is completely alone except for maybe God if they are of that persuasion.

If you sit and think quietly you will realize the depth of your own Mind and the quietness of your own Thoughts.

We all know it. We all experience the aloneness and solitude; the darkness that is our Mind. If you sit alone and think you will feel your Mind going into its deepest canyons.

The Mind is deep, dark and all encompassing.

In that deep dark cave of the Mind lies the "program" to fulfill personal needs of the being. In that deep dark cave of the Mind lies the "program" to grow in morality and in memory as choices of the being are made and things are being learned.

Note: The movie Sybil shows the depth of the Mind and what a disorder can do. The depth of the situation for some is worse because Multiple Personality Disorder or as they call it today dissociative identity disorder begins around age four before the child goes through the stage of self-actualization. For some who were born with a situation where something went wrong, their disorders began before birth offering them no opportunity to eventually remember.

In that deep dark cave of the Mind lies the "program" to form thoughts containing knowledge and to hold those Thoughts that the child had learned.

Speed of Thought

In this segment I will be referring to the speed at which we think. It is that speed that causes spontaneous inexplicable action especially in a person who has no idea why he or she behaves in a particular way. One man referred to his illness like a sneeze because he would be fine then it would hit him quickly. A sneeze comes on fast, is powerful and one has no control.

"With the speed of lightning" is the best way to describe how fast the mind works or maybe even that is way too slow.

With that incredible speed not only does the person recall and use the Thoughts it has but the Thoughts work to produce an action or a new Thought for the child to keep all within nanoseconds.

In order to do all the things we have to do, like walk as we zip our jackets, acknowledge our cold fingers, decide which way to go, walk around a hole, all the while thinking of what we want to buy for someone's birthday and where to buy it and whether that person already has that item, not to mention the fact that our eyes are looking and processing the fastest possible moving pictures and our ears are processing what we hear our Minds have to work at more than lightning speed.

How fast the Mind works is incredible especially when you think of all it has to hold while thinking of the next thing it needs to add as it assimilates, accommodates and builds schemas.

If you think of drinking a cup of coffee you can't even imagine the number of different movements and judgments you have to make with each sip. Below you will find just a very, very small list.

You have to:
Look at the cup
Send a message to your hand to grab it
Open your hand the right amount
Judge where the cup is
Place your finger in the handle of the cup
Close your hand the proper amount
Squeeze the proper amount
Lift slowly
Adjust your grip when you pick it up
Acknowledge where your mouth is
Lift it to your mouth
Place it at the proper speed toward your mouth
Judge the proper place to place it without looking
Place it at the proper place on your mouth
Perch your lips to make a seal on the cup
Lift the cup at the proper speed
Lift the cup to the proper angle
Stop lifting when the cup gets to your lips
Sip the fluid
Judge when to stop sipping
Swallow
Lower the cup

This is a list that is by far not all inclusive of the Thoughts and actions taken to simply take a drink from a cup. In addition, the person drinking is at the same time thinking and possibly talking and whatever else including using assimilation and accommodation and schema making.

The point is that Thoughts race through our Minds at an incredible rate of speed in order to allow us to function throughout the day. Thoughts already in our consciousness come to us so fast we don't realize they are happening.

That speed is often the reason that habits are so hard to break and violence or misbehavior in some people can be so spontaneous. But if we didn't think at such an incredible rate of speed we couldn't walk or talk and certainly do both at the same time while thinking of where we parked the car and that we shouldn't have worn these shoes.

According to studies it is suggested that the conscious mind processes about 2,000 bits per second while the subconscious mind processes 400 billion bits per second.

Thoughts that don't require new Thought to be built are most often automatic and unconscious. They can cause an action or a second Thought that is so fast that we don't know it's there. It is very important to know this.

An example of this situation is the man who was in prison and made friends with a female guard. Suddenly in an instant he began beating her with no knowledge of what made him do such a thing. He later stated that he liked her and had no idea why he took such an action.

After taking this action against the guard this prisoner could have been labeled with a diagnosis or an additional diagnosis of Intermittent Explosive Disorder as defined in the DSM.

In this case this man probably had an original psychiatric disorder that could be found in the DSM that should have been dealt with or he was just considered to be evil. But when you add into the equation a part of the natural mental anatomy which is the incredibly fast speed of Thought his illness suddenly caused him to attack the guard. Maybe if he knew about the speed of Thought and how it is part of "The Natural State of Being", he would have been able to adjust his thinking with his original psychological disorder and not hurt the guard.

Many DSM labeled disorders are disorders from the Psychology field like phobias for example that can be healed with psychiatry. Other disorders can be exacerbated by the things naturally found in our mental anatomy like the speed at which we think. When there is an underlying disorder, anger or frustration for example the speed of thought can cause the person to commit an act that is detrimental to the person and others.

Remember that the Thoughts throughout the day change one right after another. People often think of things but they often think much too broadly. Thoughts are small and quick and the hundreds of thousands of Thoughts if not millions or billions that happen in the day happen in a nanosecond and leave in a nanosecond as well. We need to be introspective and acknowledge the Thoughts we have throughout the day as much as we can. We need to be vigilant to be aware of the tremendous number of Thoughts we think each day or maybe be vigilant of each moment.

Memory

In "The Natural State of Being" lies Thoughts placed in the baby before birth at a time between conception and when it is viable for life in the world as part of its natural make up. Post birth behavior results from use of those Thoughts along with what is learned through living. Memory that is used with prebirth Thoughts is automatic and is not in any way conscious nor is it purposely retrievable.

The difference can be stated as preconscious purposely unretrievable memory verses conscious purposely retrievable memory. The study of memory is a field all its own. In the later chapters concerning disorders post birth memory may play a part but the part it plays is basically obvious. Memory or lack thereof, holds the key to a large part of the situation and understanding of what happened in the case of prebirth disorders only because only because the person will have no idea why they think as they do. Without being told they can't figure out what is wrong using memory.

Equilibrium

When a child's existing Thoughts in memory explain what is happening around it, it is said to be in a state of Equilibrium, a state of cognitive stability. It is in a state of balance. When the child enters a state of imbalance or disequilibrium it strives to correct this imbalance. Often the disequilibrium is caused by an imbalance that is in the unconscious Thought that was placed before birth and the Mind attempts to fix it without realizing what is happening. This drive toward equilibrium is what causes learning.

When the disequilibrium is conscious the fight for equilibrium happens as well. For some, depending the cause of the disequilibrium they simply strive for an answer they believe is there somewhere. For others, they cope somehow. This is the case with criminals whose Thought disorder causes them to think they have to kill or rape to feel better. They gain a sense of balance by accepting they are evil, denying the thought, justifying it or diving into it with cruelty.

Today there is a large-scale imbalance concerning gender. When two plus two became something else concerning gender it opened a pandoras box of imbalance. It is fine to understand that people have a disorder but when one says this disorder is how the world was made it caused a humongous disequilibrium that is only fixed when we get back to the basic truth that two plus two is four in all things and cannot be whatever we choose for it to be. That is "The Natural State of Being" concerning equilibrium.

Learning

The Thoughts placed in the Mind before birth are there to run the program for the process of learning for us to grow into autonomous adults. Swiss Psychologist Jean Piaget discovered how the process of learning works. This process that deals with learning Piaget called Assimilation and Accommodation. Without the Thoughts of Assimilation and Accommodation being placed in the Mind of the child it will learn nothing. With only Assimilation and without Accommodation the person will have only the learning that comes from repetition. In other words, the person would have to be trained. You see this in cognitively handicapped people.

When we perform a Task of using what we already know like walking, we use the schema or previously taught plan of we already know and what we do goes into memory. Assimilation is when we use the Assimilation Thought, the Thought to slightly modify or change new information to fit with our previous Thoughts. And if there is not a way the Thought could be modified to fit it causes disequilibrium, a lack of equilibrium, an instability. Accommodation Thought when the Assimilation Thought doesn't work to adjust what was taught activates to restructure or modify what we know so the new information will fit. You can study those terms more in the works of Jean Piaget but for now we will simply study learning as a series of Thoughts that have to adjust a bit since that is what learning really is.

First the child has a Thought that it thinks to be true, an already learned Thought that was placed in memory. Ler's say the child has the concept of a horse. Then it sees a picture of a zebra.

To the child the picture it sees is that of a horse that may just have stripes but it's still a horse. This would require the child to adjust its already learned Thought a bit to assimilate the new information. This new information is a striped horse.

The child is then told that is not a horse bur a zebra so the new information does not fit into the already learned Thought. This causes a slight disequilibrium. The child has to now make an adjustment in its Thought for the new information.

The Mind has to modify what was previously Thought to accommodate the new information into a new Thought.

In other words, this is the process that was set in place to change your Mind to allow you to learn new things.

It is the way we learn a new Thought and then we place it in memory.

Hold a thought while using another

An important ability in the being is the ability to hold a Thought while thinking another Thought, adding that to the original Thought and doing so again and again.

Self
The concept of "self" is another Thought in the Mind that is placed in the Prebirth stage but will not be active until much later. This concept builds as time goes on and more and more is added to the self.

The building of the self is part of "The Natural State of Being". After the child learns all that it needs to be viable, the building of the self continues on. This self-building includes Thought Concepts that we take for granted each day and are completely unconscious.

The child is a planned being. The process of carrying out the plan for the child to grow does not stop during the person's lifetime especially if something is not learned at the beginning. One example is that in "The Natural State of Being" the plan of the Thought concept of the baby turns into the Thought Concept of a toddler turns into the Thought Concept of a child turns into the Thought Concept of a teenager turns into the Thought Concept of an adult. When you think of these Thought Concepts you know what they are and even though they blend into each other in the person at first at some point they are distinct.

A baby does not move from being a toddler to being a teenager. The process is set so that moving from the planned Thought Concept from a toddler to a teenager or adult will not happen. Each is a Thought Concept with its internal series of Thought Concepts similar to the organs of the body with its cells.

Gender appears as well at some point and builds itself from a child to a boy to a man as well as from a child to a girl to a woman.

The same is true of the Thought Concepts regarding reproduction planned for later in the being's life. This includes, if all goes as planned, besides the concept of physical reproductive acts, the attraction of the person to the smile of the baby and a love for that baby as a baby which causes the promotion of the human race. This natural love of the baby is part of "The Natural State of Being".

As "The Natural State of Being" continues to do what it is programmed to do the person is growing. The only two differences between the people are what is placed as their personality and their choices.

Love and Truth

Let's say God or nature says, "I have finished constructing the body. It has all the Thoughts it needs. It is complete. It has the Thought to move the eyes at the sight of light, the Thought to suck at the touch of the lips and so on. It is built as a male or as a female. It has the physical traits linking to the look of a parent so there is a visual connection."

Then God or nature says, "I have done all I want to do. I have done enough. You do the mental part but you have to give it a Mind that is built with Love for the being and Love for all beings as well. You have been given the task of making the mental part of a human, of completing the human."

"You have been given the task of making a human Thought by Thought with each Thought connecting to the brain as a vehicle to the body. You will build the nonmaterial, invisible, unproveable world of Mind.

So, what would you put in?

Would *you* put in…

Love? The Thought of Love of self? The Thought of Love of assigned gender? The Thought of Love of talents? The Thought of Love of others? The Thought to receive Love?

Seriously, what would you put in the mind of the human? Think about it. What would you put in? Would you put in Truth so that the people would live in a stable world where all is the same and two plus two is four to all?

A bit about Love

Love is such a self-explanatory thing. Either one knows what it is or they don't.

Love of self is another Thought placed in the baby as is Love of others. These are general Thoughts. Would you put those in the human Mind?

I believe if you cared about your human, you would certainly put in Love and Truth.

Note: Some words in this book like Thought, Mind, Action Thought, Concept Thought and others have been and will be capitalized in this book. The reason is to emphasize their importance and that though they are nonmaterial they are actual entities.

III
Solving the Puzzle

CHAPTER 5
Individual Thoughts

The purpose of this chapter is to teach what Thoughts are made of and how they work.

The Mind is more powerful than the strongest and fastest computer ever made. Limitless Thoughts are being processed and stored at warp speed and we don't feel a thing. It is invisible and it is an exquisite work of pure genius.

Many state that the brain is the problem in mental illness disorders. But the brain is simply a physical vehicle for use as an intermediate between Mind and body. The Mind is connected to the body by the physical vehicle called the brain that accepts and transmits Thought messages with those messages being placed in specific designated areas.

The Mind is made of a unified group of Thoughts for the being to keep and use to grow. There are Thoughts of cause and effect; Thoughts that allow the child to adjust to unusual situations; Thoughts that allow the child to change its Mind about a Thought. There are Thoughts that have the child attempt to learn; Thoughts to be inquisitive; Thoughts for memory; there is the Thought that tells the baby it has a self; there is the Thought that tells the baby it is worthy and loved; there is a thought of equilibrium; there is the Thought that it is a human entity in the world and so on.

As you already know with the physical plan there is a mental plan, a Mind plan. The plan for the building of the physical child is perfect as is the plan for the building of the mental part of the child. The plan for each is perfect.

It needs to be stated here that post birth Thoughts can be added to a person's psyche and they can be subtracted from it as well as I am sure you already know. However, when we look for and find answers that are true, we are returning to "The Natural State of Being" where we can use all Thoughts.

I remember visiting my mother-in-law and finding her very distraught. Her very young daughter asked her why she hated her. My mother-in-law told me, "She asked me why I hated her. I told her I didn't and hugged her but what would have happened if she just thought it and never asked." I don't know where she got the word hate from to begin with but I wondered the same thing.

But even if the little girl went on thinking her mother hated her, the truth that she is loved if only by herself would have brought her back to "The Natural State of Being" because to love herself is how she was originally made.

Individual thoughts:

Each Thought placed in the unborn baby has a purpose in the child's life. Some individual Thoughts like the one where the child realizes its place in the world or the one where it realizes it is separate from other beings or the one that it has a controllable physical body are not linked to other Thoughts. Some Thoughts are "task" Thoughts that complete tasks for the child to take an action in the world. Some thoughts link with other Thoughts so the child can grow and continue to do so throughout its life. These Thoughts that were placed before birth are either general or singular Thoughts that can be pared with other Thoughts as a unit. Thoughts are called "Task Thoughts" because they complete a task. These Task Thoughts are used for the child to grow or complete a task when applied to life situations.

Example of a singular Thought

One example of a "Task Thought" that was placed to be activated sometime before the child is two years old as part of its programed order to other "Task Thoughts" is the one where the child realizes the already programmed and placed concept "that they exist separately from the objects and people around them". I am using this one example to show you how intricate Thoughts are, and how it would seem unthinkable that this Thought has to be placed in the child at all. But, of course, it does.

Every single thing we do no matter how fast, unconscious, big or little we do it because of a Thought in our Minds. Every single thing. No matter how general, broad, detailed, minute, hidden, deep, profound, intense, overt or covert the action is it originates from a Thought.

Each physical cell has a Task Thought placed in it as part of its instruction so it knows what to do. For instance, cells like white blood cells, are given the job of cleaning the blood of foreign objects and will work aggressively to do so. Those cells do not have the Task Thought to do anything but clean nor do they have the same Task Thought as other Task Thoughts like the Thoughts in the cell to beat in unison as in the case of a heart cell or make other cells as in the case of bone marrow.

Multiple Singular Thoughts that work as one:

Some single though connected Thoughts are sequenced to be used one after another. Toward the task of learning, with the Thoughts that are used as one the process is as follows. The attempt at Assimilation of a concept (the Thought to change the situation just a bit) is followed by Accommodation when Assimilation doesn't work. When Assimilation doesn't work the process begins that will change the Mind. It is the process of Assimilation, Equilibration (the Thought to make things right), then Accommodation (the Thought to change the existing Thought) then the Thought to place the new concept in memory.

Another example of one Thought following a sequence after another is the Thought of ego centricity, a Thought the child is born with where it is centered on itself and the feelings of another are not considered. Later this Thought of ego centricity is replaced with the Thought of empathy bit by bit as the child matures into an adult.

For better understanding of how the Thought process as part of "The Natural State of Being" works, I will give you an example of the Thoughts related to how we learn as discovered by Psychologist Jean Piaget. I will be explaining the Thought series that is part of the cognitive process that is used to take in new information.

Below is an example of the two connected Thoughts that work together to complete the task of learning something called Assimilation and Accommodation. This explanation goes as follows:

First the child has the already realized concept of what a horse is in its Mind because it had been taught that that is a horse.

The word horse refers to the image of the object that is a horse that the child remembers.

Then the child sees a zebra. It thinks that it is a horse mainly because it looks like one and that is already the remembered concept in the child's Mind so it adjusts a little bit. The concept is a bit different but it has all the features of a horse so it is a horse. It is a horse with stripes to the child.

Someone says, "That's not a horse. It's a zebra. See the stripes?"

The child now has a new concept of what the picture is and has to "accommodate" or adjust the previous remembered concept of a horse since the previous thought is incorrect in this instance and the object was not a horse.

The child then has to change its previous concept that this is a zebra changing its Mind about the old information to make it new information.

The new information becomes a new concept that this is a zebra and that new concept is placed in memory.

Now in the child's Mind there is the Thought of a horse and the Thought of a zebra.

Assimilation and Accommodation happens throughout a person's life. I am going to give you the adult post birth version of the same process.

Say there was a woman who had a brother-in-law. She considered him family and had no doubt of that status. Every time he came over to her house, he brought a bouquet of flowers and kissed her on the cheek and asked how his favorite sister-in-law was doing. The already believed Thought was that he is a really nice family-oriented guy.

One day the woman goes to dinner with her friend and at dinner she sees him with a woman who is not her sister.

She adjusts or assimilates her thoughts to make sense of it using her already remembered Thoughts. "Hmmm, he must be here on a break from work with his coworker". The woman assimilates her Thought to make sense of what she just saw using what she already believed to be true that the brother-in-law was a nice family-oriented guy.

The brother-in-law leans over and kisses the woman at his table affectionately as they get up to leave. This contradiction between what she thought of him and what she could not deny caused her to have to accommodate what she saw through the realization that the brother-in-law was not what she previously thought. That new Thought concerning the brother-in-law is now placed in memory.

She has to Accommodate for what she saw with a new concept about her brother-in-law that contradicts the old concept that her brother-in-law is a nice family guy. This new concept is placed in memory and she has learned.

That is an instance of how we learn as adults, provided we don't get stuck in the Assimilating step over and over again which Sigmund Freud would call denial! Just kidding…sort of!

These few examples of Thoughts that are placed in the unborn baby deal with learning. These are, of course, only a few of so many prebirth Thoughts and, as stated before, they are completely unknown to the baby and the adult.

More Thoughts in the learning Scenario

Most think Assimilation and Accommodation are the only thoughts in the Thought set of learning. But Piaget also uncovered the Thought of Equilibrium which would of course also include its counterpart of disequilibrium. I discovered the two basic parts that work together in every Thought like the parts that make up an atom. And those parts are made of Thought as well. They are the Thoughts that keep the concept and the Thoughts that take the Action.

Here we will go through the learning process again with the addition of the Thought of Equilibrium or more accurately stated disequilibrium and the Thoughts of Concept and Action.

First the child already has the concept of what a horse is in its Mind because it had been taught the concept that that image of a horse refers to the object that is a horse.

The Action had already been taken that placed that concept of a horse in the child's memory for later recall.

Then the child sees a zebra. It thinks that it, too, is a horse mainly because it looks like one and that is already the placed concept in the child's Mind so it adjusts a little bit. It Assimilates which is an Action to change the concept that that object, though a bit different, is a horse. To the child it is a horse with stripes.

Someone says, "That's not a horse. It's a zebra. See the stripes?"

Slight disequilibrium occurs making the child's Mind take the Action to remedy the situation and make things right meaning bring things back to the state of equilibrium.

Since the previous remembered concept in this instance is incorrect that that was not a horse, the child's Mind has to accommodate for the situation by making a new concept that it is a zebra. It uses the Accommodation concept that it has to change the idea of the horse. The child then has to change, which is to take an action, its previous concept that this is a zebra. It uses the concept that it can change its Mind and takes the Action to do so. Now the thought is changed its Mind about the old information to make it into new information.

The new information becomes a new concept that this is a zebra and that concept is placed in memory. Placing a Thought in memory is an action.

Now in the child's Mind there is the Thought of a horse and the Thought of a zebra.

Now here is the adult version of the brother-in-law story showing equilibrium or disequilibrium, concept and action.

Again, there was a woman who had a brother-in-law. She considered him family and had no doubt of that status. Every time he came over to her house, he brought a bouquet of flowers and kissed her on the cheek and asked how his favorite sister-in-law was doing. The already believed thought concept was that he is a really nice family-oriented guy.

One day the woman goes to dinner with her friend and at dinner she sees him with a woman who is not her sister.

Disequilibrium sets in. She unconsciously takes the action to assimilate her thoughts to make sense of it using the assimilation concept. "Hmmm, he must be here on a break from work with his coworker." The woman tries get back to the state of equilibrium to make sense of what she just saw using what she already believed to be true that the brother-in-law was a nice family-oriented guy with the unconscious assimilation Thought.

The brother-in-law leans over and kisses the woman at his table affectionately as they get up to leave. This contradiction between what she thought of him and what she could not deny causes a disequilibrium in her thinking. She now accommodates meaning forms a new concept of the brother-in-law. That new Thought concerning the brother-in-law is now placed in memory. Now with this new understanding she returns to the state of equilibrium.

(This process of changing one's Mind in order to learn is called Assimilation and Accommodation by psychologist Jean Piaget which you can read about in his research.)

That process of how we learn is a schema or plan of connected thoughts toward one goal. It is also how we learn as children and as adults, provided we don't get stuck in the Assimilating step over and over again which Sigmund Freud would call denial! Just kidding...sort of!

Schema.

Without Thoughts we could not learn. We certainly would not walk. There are Thoughts that are connected and run in tandem to each other or are sequential. The above scenarios where multiple Thoughts are connected show the single plan in these sequential Thought sets as they work as one to complete a task which is to learn. The Thought plan used when they work together is called a Schema. It is the plan for the Thought actions toward a single goal. These Thoughts are planted in the Mind of the child...AS ONE UNIT.

These "units" are brought from memory repeatedly throughout the day. Besides the "unit" of Thoughts used for learning as I have already shown you there are, of course, so many others. For example, let's take the task of walking. When you walk from one place to another so very many Thoughts are in play. There are the Thoughts of where you are going, how to get there and so on. We will be talking about the simple task of physically walking.

The baby first walks learning to balance, to put one foot in front of the other, to lift its foot the right amount, to place its foot the right amount of distance from the body and so on. All of this learning is placed in memory. Eventually it learns to move its foot at the correct angle so it is not unbalanced and wobbly and it will walk as we walk.

Using the Thought of Accommodation in the learning Thought unit causes the child to learn to walk as an adult would walk and these new Thoughts are placed in memory along with the old already learned Thoughts. This forms a unit...a walking unit.

The set of Thoughts that go together that are one unit that are in memory are recalled so we can walk. This unit of Thoughts can be adjusted as we use the Thoughts in a unit if we trip and have to change our actions to keep from falling. We then go back to the single unit of Thoughts that are used for walking.

We use these Thought sets or "Thought Units" with their planted schema going from one "Thought Unit" to another all day long with incredible speed without any knowledge of it happening. Even the Thought set of how to keep from falling is in itself a "Thought Unit".

We use these "Thought Units" for grabbing, drinking, walking, talking, scratching, eating, looking...you get the point.

CHAPTER 6
Anatomy of the Individual Thought/The Second Revelation

The purpose of this chapter is to teach that there are two components to each Thought.

It was here that I realized that a Thought was not just a Thought. After studying Thoughts and the connected Thoughts and how they operate I realized what would become a large part of the answer to mental illness though I didn't realize it at the time. It became obvious that each Thought had its own parts. Thoughts were not simply just Thoughts. Like the cell or atom there was more to the picture than what seemed to be.

Task Thoughts are made of united Concept Thoughts and Action Thoughts both of which are required for the task Thought to work as it should. One example is if the child has acquired the Concept Thought that it "exists separately from the objects and people around" that Concept Thought needs an Action Thought and that Action Thought is to mentally realize the Concept Thought. In other words, the child applies the Concept of being separate from the objects and people around it meaning that is now a physical "self".

If you include placing a Thought in memory or realizing it or practicing it or choosing to reflect or practice the Thoughts in "The Natural State of Being" then every Thought has the same two basic components and it may be that every Thought is a Task Thought whether conscious or not.

Some Thoughts simply do what is in "The Natural State of Being". They are the Thoughts to receive and express love or receive and express truth. They basically get out of the way. All Thoughts that get things done are Task Thoughts that complete a task whether it is general or specific and whether it is significant of insignificant whether it is conscious or not. Just as the body can live without a limb or an eye but not without a heart or brain the Mind has components that are just for use or completely needed for survival.

This discovery of the innerworkings of each Thought led to the discovery of the cause of mental illness.

At times one has to dive deep into the world of atoms to understand the cells and the workings of the body as one has to dive deep into the components of Thought to understand the workings of the Mind.

As the atom consists of protons and neutrons the "Task Thought" or any Thought in the Mind consists of parts as well. The normal properly functioning and properly placed Thought has two components.

The components of the "Task Thought" or any Thought are Concept and Action components and they are Thoughts as well. The "Task Thought" or any Thought in the Mind is made of these two Thoughts acting in unison or as a Unit.

As you are reading this you are using the "Task Thoughts" of Assimilation and Accommodation and placing the Thoughts you have learned into memory. The "Task Thoughts" were placed in the baby before birth and were meant to be used by the being for the purpose of learning and doing things throughout its life. Though you are using the Thoughts of Assimilation and Accommodation, memory placement and schema building at this very moment you cannot feel them being used nor can you stop them from being used.

The breaking down of the individual Thought is key to understanding the Mind and the disorders that occur due to injury before purposely retrievable memory is formed. The "Task Thoughts" that are placed in the child before birth are put there to become activated at the time specified in its preplanned programming. Though some believe the Thoughts are put there later after the child is born, I have no doubt they are put there before birth and activated at the proper time according the proper sequence and programming. This would explain child prodigies.

Before I tell you the things you need to know about the Mind and the disorders you need to understand how the two parts that make up Thoughts effect not only the mental world but the actual world as well. Therefore, I will take you through a real-life scenario. This will help you understand the components of the Thoughts that are part of Mind and "The Natural State of Being".

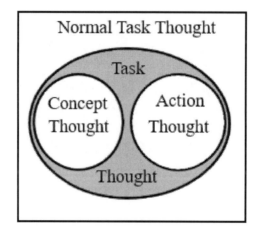

I V
Uncovering Mystery of Mysteries that will Never be Solved

CHAPTER 7
Missing Thought Component/The Third Revelation

"…The point is discovering them" - Galileo

The purpose of this chapter is to teach that one of the two components that make up one Thought could be missing

A hypothetical Concept Thought/Action Thought scenario:

It's Sunday night. The "Task" that has to be completed is to take the garbage can to the curb so it will be picked up on Monday morning. You have a teenager and it is that teenager's job to take out the garbage on Sunday night for Monday morning pick up.

You come down the stairs and say to the teenager who is sitting on the couch. "It's Sunday night, you know." The teenager knows the garbage has to go out. He has that Concept but just sits there and takes no Action.

Without the Action to take out the garbage will the garbage go out?

No.

Now you have a different scenario. Let's say you come down the stairs on a Sunday night and there is a different teenager who has the task of taking the garbage out, a girl for ease of understanding. You say, "Go do it."

She stands and sits and stands and sits and takes the Action as best she can. But she has no clue what you are talking about because she doesn't have the Concept that the garbage has to go out.

Will the garbage go out?

No.

So, the person needs the Concept Thought that the garbage cans need to go out and the person needs to have the Action Thought because an action needs to be taken. The Concept and Action are needed to get the garbage cans out to the curb for Monday pick up.

Concept and Action were needed to complete that Task and any task and Concept and Action need to work together as a unit for the task to be completed and the garbage cans get to the curb for Monday pick up. Therefore, each "Task Thought" that completes a task is made up of a Concept Thought and an Action Thought as one unit that are separate yet work together to complete each task.

You have been given the general aspects of the Mind such as speed, depth and learning. You have also been given information on the programming that makes up the Mind of the being and the plan that is "The Natural State of Being.

But to understand what is really going on one has to dive deeper into the Mind which means understanding the individual Thought and understanding what the individual Thought is actually made of. Without breaking down the individual Thought into its components one cannot understand not only the Mind but the disorders that occur from injuries that happen before birth of consciously retrievable memory is formed.

The brain has no place in the world of Mind as it is a physical thing and is part of the physical medical field. All things psychological or mental deal with the Mind.

The body is made up of cells just as the Mind is made up of Thoughts. There are enough cells for the body to use just as there are enough Thoughts for the Mind to use and they are all part of "The Natural State of Being". The cells are enormous in number. The Thoughts, though we can't see or feel them are also enormous in number.

The inside of the cell that is in the body is made of atoms. The cell can contain many atoms. The inside of the Thought in the Mind unlike the many atoms in the cell is less complicated and is merely a union of only two connected Thoughts. "Task Thoughts" which make up most if not all Thoughts are the Thoughts that are in the Mind that are responsible for the person using their mentality to accomplish tasks using the body. Inside the "Task Thought" is a union of two Thoughts that, unless something goes wrong, work as one.

Inside the "Task Thought" is a union of two connected Thoughts with one Thought in the "Task Thought" union being the Concept Thought and the other being the Action Thought. In the "Task Thought" union the Concept Thought tells the "Task Thought" what is to be done and Action Thought of the union takes the action to get the job done.

Thoughts to be placed in the Mind of the unborn baby are meticulously designed as part of its programming.

These "Task Thoughts" and all Thoughts are infused into the brain as tea would be infused in water. They are throughout the brain and can sometimes be mapped such as thoughts of compassion being in the frontal lobe. And as stated earlier the brain is the vehicle for use of the body.

It has to be noted that the Thought of Equilibrium is also a task Thought. The concept is that things must make sense. The action is to search for the answer that will make whatever was presented to the child or adult make sense. The world that makes sense is "The Natural state of Being". This state makes it so all humans are standing on the same stable ground and can relate to each other on that stable ground.

Any disruption in the placement of the designed Thoughts at the time before birth will make the person do things without knowing the cause for their actions. Detrimental Thoughts could result from this damage that can last for the entire life of the person. Sometimes the detrimental Thoughts will not be acted upon until later in life.

The person cannot fix their individual damaged Thoughts because there was no prior healthy Thought available. In other words, there was no memory of what should be the natural life-building healthy Thought for comparison. Because of this the person can get into situations where they do horrendous things without knowing why like become a serial killer or fear killer or have a commonly known disorder like Autism or Schizophrenia.

An element is one of the simplest parts of which anything consists. The element of speed of Thought in the above case is one of the millions of elements made of Thoughts that make up the mental anatomy of the human being.

What I am giving you from here is over forty plus years' worth of education, contemplation, study and research…the Grey's Anatomy of the Mind.

Appreciate what you have here and know that the answers which have eluded professionals in the psychiatric world, the religious world and the forensic world are forever at your fingertips.

I did all the work. I did all the research. I did all the diving into horrors of serial killings and painful disorders to get these answers for you. I listened to the cries of parents of not only those who were victims but of the perpetrators.

By the time this book came to the point where syndromes were to be written, I was exhausted. In order to go on I had to watch true stories of crimes that were solved to push me to continue. I was so tired especially trying to get to the deepest Thoughts in the syndromes that I had to sleep after only a few hours of work.

So, treasure what you are about to learn. Embrace it. It will save lives.

As of this writing most of the disorders I discovered were due to missing a "Task Thought". I worked for many years with students who, I had learned, had Thoughts that were missing. I worked with a young lady named Jodi who had missing "Task Thought" of Accommodation making her cognitively handicapped and unable to learn.

But as many who work in the field of special education know, students often have more than one issue, more than one disability. Jodi also had speech problems. She had the complete "Task Thought" including the Concept Thought and Action Thought union concerning the Thought that one speaks by making noise. But she didn't have the complete set of "Task Thoughts" allowing her to speak because she was missing either the Concept Thought or Action Thought dealing with the Thought that words connect to symbols. Therefore, she made vocal noises when she wanted something, but used no actual words.

Chapter 8
More than just a missing Thought/The Fourth Revelation

Purpose: to teach the disorders that happen when one part of the Thought is missing.

At this point in time, I was still studying people who had the one particular disorder that caused them to believe they needed to do terrible things like kill to relieve the feeling caused by the disorder. I knew there were so many who had the first disorder I discovered and I knew there was a drive that would bring some to the point of complete destruction, but I didn't know what the drive was. I had to understand the full impact of this loss on people to know the depth of the first disorder I discovered and why it drove people to such extreme measures that would destroy their lives and the lives of others. I had to know why it had such an impact that it made people do the most horrendous things. Sometimes they would also then kill themselves, which made no sense until I got the answers I needed.

The answer came from a man who was a young very intelligent medical student, who was a person with a genius IQ who was a mass murderer. He stated that the killings he did were supposed to increase his self-worth and that taking lives added to his own value. He also said that what the victim did gets canceled and goes to him. This was so revealing.

I found that this kind of statement, though in each person's own words, was repeated over and over again by others I had studied. The normal person has their own "value" for lack of a better term and does not have to take from another. If a person has to take from another to fulfill themselves, something has to be missing. One cannot fill the cup twice. It has to be emptied to be refilled.

It was the study of this very intelligent highly educated young man that led me to understand that there was a missing piece in the first place. This person also said that there was no choice but to kill or commit suicide. This shows the extreme depth of the disorder, the belief that there was no other way and the drive behind it. Another person I studied who took similar actions led me to understand what the missing Thought specifically was.

Disorders found in Thoughts that were imbedded before birth.

There are disorders of the brain where the brain is not, or is no longer, a good conductor for the Thoughts in the Mind. Disorders of the Mind are different from disorders of the brain. Often, if not always, disorders of the brain cause it to simply work slowly or, in particular areas, not work at all. Disorders of the Mind are not seen in an autopsy, but can only be revealed by the behavior of the person. They cannot be seen at all.

Though further research may find more causes for disorders that began before birth, so far what was found is that the current recorded disorders are caused by a Thought that was supposed to be placed in the unborn baby, but was not.

The situation in which a "Task Thought" or any Thought for that matter, that was supposed to be placed in the Mind of the unborn baby but was not, leaves the person with no memory of any time prior.

This situation leaves them with no memory of Thoughts to the contrary as they were not there from the beginning. A person would have absolutely no reference in order to change their Thought. There would be no knowledge that there had been anything different, until living in the world proves it to be so and the Mind's drive pushes for action.

When you realize the age of the onset of a Prebirth disorder, you get a better perspective of the depth of the disorder and the hold it has on the being.

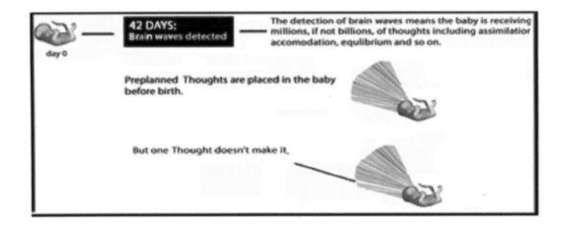

The person would have no background to rely on to understand anything except for what they thought their entire lives. There would be a tremendous emptiness. This is the cause of those with any disorder in this stage to say they were "born this way" and psychiatrists to say the person had "a terrible emptiness, a void".

Those who have something go wrong with any prebirth imbedded Thoughts would say and have said, "I live in another dimension" or "I live on the other side of the window" or "I knew I was different" or "I knew there was something missing when I was seven" or "I have a broken brain" and so on.

Three things can happen when there is a missing prebirth Thought. The first is that the "Task Thought" or any Thought, for that matter, is completely missing.

The second thing that can happen, when there is a disorder that happens before birth, is that there is a missing Action Thought, part of the "Task Thought" union, with the Concept Thought part intact. Without Action the "Task Thought" would not be acted upon and might as well be nonexistent. The task, of course, would not be completed. In some instances, the child won't know it is missing and there would be no emptiness and no severe drive.

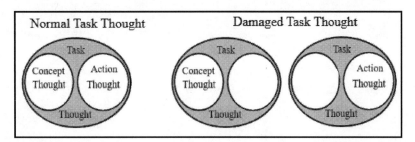

The third thing that can go wrong before birth is that the Concept Thought part of the "Task Thought" is missing, but the Action Thought is intact. The first two situations simply cause a person to be unable to function depending on what the Thought is that is missing, making the person simply disabled.

If the Concept Thought of the "Task Thought" union is missing, it is a whole different story. The Action part does its job, which means it fights to make the Concept Thought work, to make the "Task Thought" do its job and get the task completed since the two parts, the Concept Thought and Action Thought are unified.

Prebirth disorders are caused when the Thoughts that are supposed to be placed in the unborn baby are not placed. Damage that occurs before birth can cause a variety of disorders depending on when the damage occurs and what Thought is being placed at that time.

Some disorders do not cause pain to the person, especially if the Action Thought is not fighting back, while others cause severe mental pain and an extreme need to relieve the pain. When speaking of the missing Thoughts and the behaviors believed that needed to be taken to relieve the pain, one man said, "If I didn't give into them, I would be crushed by them."

The loss of the Concept Thought can cause what could be likened to a cytokine storm which is well known in the medical field. For those who do not know what that is, it is an immune system overreaction triggered by infection, faulty genes or autoimmune disorders. When the body has something happen to it, sometimes the body's response will be to overreact, causing the body to fight back with a vengeance to the detriment of its own health. That is a cytokine storm.

In a similar way when the Mind tries to use the Concept Thought and cannot, it often responds with a vengeance. It may simply be responding normally, which would itself cause a reaction and a drive, or, it can overrespond as in a cytokine storm. Either one would explain why some with particular prebirth disorders say the need to react comes on "like a sneeze". In either case, the reaction is beyond powerful.

There are many Thoughts placed before purposefully retrievable memory is formed. There are many Thoughts that can be blocked or stopped for various reasons. The first syndrome I discovered is one disorder that happens before birth that causes a "Task Thought" to be unable to do its job. But there are so many others depending on the Thought that was supposed to be placed. I have seen and heard the most horrendous stories in my research due to the first disorder I was studying. One man who had a prebirth disorder killed a child then took a knife and stabbed himself in the neck until he died.

I would listen to the statements and feelings of family members of those who killed or raped, who had no idea their loved one was anything but normal and had no idea why their loved one acted as he/she did. They were traumatized and often moved away to escape.

One man whose behavior was truly horrendous said he knew something was missing when he was seven-years-old. Since this situation began before birth, such a statement would make perfect sense. I heard the recording of him saying this and realized what should have been obvious… it hits the children. I groaned, causing someone to ask me if I was ok. I said I was, but I was not.

By now, I had been studying this situation for five years. Those who cared to understand what I was doing were no longer interested and, in their defense, no longer wanted to take the confusing journey with me since it was growing and changing all the time. My body, after sitting in front of a computer listening and writing, had deteriorated as had my health. I was stiff and I was very tired.

Today, I am mostly afraid now that I know how many there are with these disorders, the severity of these disorders and what people will do for relief. Maybe you could say I'm now cautious. I think sometimes of the movie "Taken" where the daughter of the CIA operative says, "Mom says your job made you paranoid." He replies, "No, my job made me aware."

Today I am absolutely aware. I am also tired, worn out, and probably a bit boring to be around. But more than anything I am grateful for the gift of understanding that I was given. And when I feel alone with this heavy burden on my shoulders I think, "This is not my job. This is God's job. I am merely a conduit, a messenger. Then I can take a breath and wait for the next step.

The story for all with disorders that are before birth started with an injury that happened from the time of conception to about 20 weeks of gestation. I believe this injury is caused by a slight lack of oxygen to the tiniest maybe even microscopic fetus or embryo that I call a baby. This injury causes a disability due to the loss of a Thought that should have been placed in the baby to be used as its "Natural State of Being" but was not placed. As the child goes through life, its Mind tries to use the missing Thought, but it cannot. Sometimes the missing Thought is one that has to do with intelligence and the being simply stays unaware of the loss its entire life. For those who are cognizant of something so very wrong, the loss often causes mental pain.

When you have a series of stories and pleas from those with specific behaviors and the number of those stories and pleas increases the more it is researched the fact that there is a disorder becomes obvious.

About five years ago, I accidently discovered there was a mental disorder that made people do things they normally wouldn't do and, more importantly, they did not want to do and could not explain. It sometimes even made them commit suicide.

General Symptoms of those with prebirth disorders

When there is a disorder that began before birth, often you will find similar symptoms. Not all prebirth disorders have all the symptoms shown. Some have other symptoms, especially if both Concept Thought and Action Thought are missing.

Symptom 1: They don't want the disorder or its behaviors.

The behavior of people with disorders that started before birth can vary from mild, slightly life altering, to behavior that is severely dangerous to themselves or others and all degrees in between, depending on the specific disorder. Those with disorders that started before birth often behave in a manner that is hard for those without a prebirth disorder to understand.

A person with the missing cognitive Thought that has to do with completing a task, may suddenly get up and run. This is the Action Thought of the "Task Thought" union acting as it should to complete the task without the Concept Thought to tell the being what to get up and do. Rocking or spontaneously running is a symptom of a prebirth disorder where the Concept Thought is missing and the Action Thought is taking over. Often, you will see a person who spontaneously rocks or runs do so, stop, wait, rock or run again throughout the day as the Action Thought repeatedly kicks in.

On the other hand, when there is cognizance, it is a different story. Being cognizant that something is wrong or missing, the Action Thought is still fighting, but in this case, the person is aware there is something very wrong.

Those with prebirth disorders can have high intelligence, normal intelligence or low intelligence, with their ability to know something is wrong still intact. If the person is cognizant that something is wrong, they will most often feel an incredibly strong need to fix the problem, just as the person with no cognizance, no awareness of their disorder unconsciously tries to fix the problem by rocking or running.

There are some prebirth disorders that do not have an Action Thought driving them and in these instances the person has a missing Concept Thought and a missing Action Thought. If the Thought missing is one of Love for others this person will be able to do things like hurt others without any remorse. These people are considered to have no conscience. With these people, loss of Equilibrium may cause additional issues but not usually.

There are a few prebirth disorders that make a person feel as though they have to kill or hurt another person to relieve that particular disorder and fill that particular loss. If the perceived way to fix the problem is to hurt another person, they often try to fight it as long as possible to no avail and eventually give in, sometimes through hurting someone and sometimes through suicide. They don't want whatever the disorder is, are often very pained by it and try to seek help in differing ways. They want it to go away, so that they can live a normal life. Since it is there from birth, though, they often eventually simply accept it.

Symptom 2: They have no control.

Those with a disorder of which they are not cognizant will react in unusual ways with no idea of why and maybe even no idea that they are acting in unusual ways at all. A being with one particular prebirth disorder will spontaneously run, flap their hands, make unintelligible noises to name a few behaviors. Some with a different prebirth disorder will simply live a solitary life with no desire or need for social activity. Some will do what is seen as extremely selfish; some will hurt others or themselves.

Due to the depth of the disorder and the lack of understanding of what the disorder is, the person has no control to stop the feeling the disorder brings and will try to do dangerous things to deal with the feeling, no matter what the cost. If they are cognizant of their world and that there is something wrong, they will often seek help, but their pleas for help go unanswered.

As I stated before, prebirth disorders are different for each of the Syndromes. Some are major disrupters of life causing pain that ripples to others and some cause pain basically to only the sufferer. Some disorders are very mild and hardly noticed in the life of the person. Some destroy it. Some people have more than one Syndrome making their lives much more difficult to explain.

One set of people with a specific prebirth disorder. would hurt people though their deep desire would be not to do so. "Please stop me. I cannot control myself". "I can't help what I did…" "When I did what I did I was sick. I hope I can be cured…" In 1861 one man said he could not help what he did "…no more than the poet can help the inspiration to sing". When speaking of his behavior of killing others and being cognizant of it, one man from England said, "…I know that and I feel for them, but it doesn't mean I won't do it again."

People with prebirth disorders may be able to heal if they know they have a prebirth disorder. If they do not know what they have, they will be driven by the disorder with no control over the behavior the disorder suggests would bring them relief.

Another man, who felt he had to kill to relieve his pain and not wanting to do any more damage to people, turned himself in to the police saying to them in his own words that he turned himself in to avoid hurting others. He stated that when he did what he did he was sick and he hoped he could be cured while incarcerated. He died in prison having never been cured.

My studies took me not only back in time, but to very faraway places. But I didn't have to go far to find more and more with the same disorder. They were everywhere. All over our country. All over other countries.

One man called it a monster and said he never knew when it entered his brain but it was there to stay and he can't stop it. It is called many names but mostly it is called the monster.

The truth is, of course, that though they have a powerful drive to kill or hurt another, they can make a choice not to by suicide, an action some take or by getting arrested and spending life in prison. That would have been the heroic thing to do and I know of some who took that route.

Symptom 3: They have no knowledge of why they behave as they do.

Those who are not cognizant of their behavior would obviously have no idea why they behave as they do and, unless they are told, they may not know something is wrong. It stands to reason that one with a disorder that has to do with intelligence such as one who has the loss of Assimilation or Accommodation, would have little or no ability to do things of intelligence, and certainly no knowledge of why they were as they were, and possibly little or no cognizance that they are different from others at all.

There are those who have intelligence in the normal or above normal range who do things that to them are inexplicable. When asked about his behavior one man who had a genius IQ said, "smarter men than me have tried to figure that out."

Symptom 4: Have behavior that is often misunderstood.

I worked in many facilities and many homes in my career with special students. So many times, a student's behavior was misunderstood by the person in charge and I often thought it futile to correct the mistaken person. The latest was a fifty-year-old Down Syndrome lady who was just taken from her mother who was dying and put in a home. She was desperate to make a necklace of beads for her mother and made many of them. The "behaviorist" said she was "perseverating" and he instructed others to take her beads away. All she was trying to do was make something to insure she saw her mother again. One man took her beads and hid them, causing her to go into a panic and try to run out the door. Later, on the way home, this same man told her she would never see her mother again. What this lady was doing made perfect sense if she was seen as a person. But she wasn't.

On the other side of the spectrum, there were those with prebirth disorders who had normal or above normal intelligence who were misunderstood, I heard the testimonies of Psychiatrists and Psychologists as they placed labels on those with prebirth disorders who committed crimes. Most times the labels were for court purposes.

Often those who committed crimes and were caught, suddenly saw shadows or hallucinated when it was not reported before. This is simply a way of recording this concept in case it is needed for an insanity plea later. Many psychologists used these to present a diagnosis.

But worse than that, when a person was caught and in prison, the person would often try to tell what really happened and what the problem was in a last-ditch effort to do at least some good and save another from the same fate. Though some were sincere, many reporters, who it seemed were mostly in the interview for the sensationalism or a slight unrealized revenge, completely missed the mark on what the criminal was saying as did many other law enforcement officials.

Without understanding "The Natural State of Being" which explains prebirth disorders those who are supposed to provide understanding will not be able to do so accurately or at all resulting in the disorders that cause such destruction to be called, "The Mystery of Mysteries that will Never be Solved".

Symptom 5: They have the same symptoms as so many others.

The numbers I found were staggering. I researched only one disorder at first because that disorder was what led me to the discovery of "The Natural State of Being" and prebirth epistemic psychology. As I studied this disorder, I found a huge number of people with symptoms like the symptoms of the first subject who felt the need to kill others and therefore I realized it was the same disorder. This was a stunning revelation. I had pages and pages of names as I had already told you.

Because I would do research on my phone when I was not at my computer, more and more stories of people with this disorder popped up. Of course, I had to look. The number of people who had the same disorder that made the person think they needed to kill to relieve the pain was a complete shock. Instead of a few, I found hundreds who basically said, "I was hoping not" when it came to their killing behavior. I knew I could have found thousands if I looked longer.

My students who had a prebirth disorder that affected intellect, simply lived their lives and often did so happily, having no realization of the loss they were living. I never felt compelled to dig any deeper than I already had for them. But in the cases of people like the first two subjects, people were hurting and other people were being hurt, sometimes seriously. I had to know more.

Knowing very little about people who had normal or higher IQs who also had what seemed to be a developmental disability, forced me to fight to understand prebirth disorders in those without cognitive problems that caused people to do things for what seems to be no logical reason, with no control and without knowing why. This is common knowledge when referring to those with intellectual developmental disabilities. Often, we just expect these things of such people.

Prebirth disorders in those with a normal to high IQ are usually misunderstood. There are as many disorders as there are individual Thoughts in the being. Most go unnoticed because they are so minute.

Bizarre and sometimes dangerous behavior for no logical reason in those having no control over this behavior and having no idea why, led to the discovery that these behaviors are caused by a prebirth disorder. Researching the situation in the first and second situations and the people's symptoms, revealed hundreds more with the same symptoms and also revealed more symptoms. More symptoms arose and more answers were revealed toward the discovery of "The Natural State of Being" and prebirth disorders and the many syndromes from those disorders.

When I finally learned what the details of the disorders that happened in the Mind before birth were, how "The Natural State of Being" played a role and the breakdown of the Task Thoughts into Concept Thought and Action Thought, I understood all the pieces of the puzzle. I understood why people with these disorders feel they live in another world or dimension, why some feel the need to kill or hurt another or commit suicide, why they feel no remorse for their behavior yet would cry at the testimonies of the families of people they hurt, why they needed to keep being reminded of their behavior and much more will be understood, as each disorder is uncovered and explained. Revelation after revelation brought answers to all the questions and a path to understanding the disorders, and the world of prebirth Mind.

What truly brought about understanding of the disorders and prebirth epistemic psychology, was the intense drive that caused these people to do such incredibly bizarre, heinous and sometimes dangerous things and the reason that need was there. Understanding why they were and are driven by a powerful force they had no idea existed was understood when "The Natural State of Being and prebirth epistemic psychology and its aspects was explained.

I will explain it simplistically for now so you can understand the symptoms, but it does get deeper.

Symptom 6: They often try to understand why they do what they do.

This symptom relates to those who have the cognition to know that something is wrong. Those with disorders of intellect have no ability to heal themselves, nor do they try to, as they are not aware something is wrong, nor do they have the   that it would be healable. There are those with prebirth disorders and those with other disorders who simply accept having their disorder and go on with their lives. What is missing simply is accepted or maybe fought for a bit, given up on and then accepted.

Symptoms of prebirth disorders run the gamut from those with low cognition who are kind and accepting to those with high cognition who can be dangerous as they try to relieve their mental pain. As I studied and listened to the words only of those whose disorder caused behavior that was life destroying in one way or another, I found that many with prebirth disorders and the cognizance to know there was something wrong or missing were searching for the reasons and a cure for their disorder. Often, they would jump from this reason to that reason swearing what they thought about why they behaved as they did was correct, only to realize that it wasn't.

Symptom 7: They feel they live in another Dimension and they actually do.

The depth of the prebirth disorders is one that is very hard to explain. When this particular disorder hits, which can go from being an all day long every day thing to being about 1% of the person's day, it is all-encompassing. It is like the intense darkness when there is no light available at all for those with particular disorders.

Though her disorder was after memory was formed and the cause of her disability was not remembered until later, the movie Sybil does a great job unveiling the depths of things in the dimension of prebirth disorders as well. For your information Sybil and her doctor, Dr. Wilbur, were like mother and daughter the rest of their lives and Sybil, whose real name was Shirley Mason, said it happened just as the book stated.

A great description of what it is like to have a prebirth disorder that makes one feel like they live in another dimension came from Sol Pais. Sol Pais was still a teenager when she attempted to shoot up schools in Denver. When she failed, she ran through the woods with her pump action shotgun and shot herself in the head, which killed her instantly. The reporters said her writing was filled with angst. That must have been some angst. In her angst filled journals she said, "I live in another dimension". The thing is that Sol really did live in another dimension. Her Prebirth disorder was basically located in another dimension and she revisited it each time she unconsciously tried to use the particular missing Thought. This journey through another dimension was one that began before birth and stayed in her Mind because it was before memory was formed. The depth and loneliness of this disorder is all the sufferers know. The loss from this disorder is all encompassing. The emptiness is powerful and comes on with the force of a sneeze and sometimes just as quickly.

This is Sol Pais. I left her picture in this book, so that you could see the sadness on her face. She was able to explain what it was like to have this particular disorder from a female's very creative point of view. I learned of the depth of the first disorder that I discovered from her. And when you understand you will see it was another dimension because it was so hidden and it was a place her Mind unconsciously went to all the time. It was the dimension of someone continually being tossed into a world where there is no understanding and where no one else exists.

It was the dimension where the missing thought was. Just as one man said its other side of the window, another man said, "I felt so completely different having to live in a world of people who were not like me". Another man said, somewhat inaccurately, he was two different people.

The reason it was another dimension is because these people kept being thrown back into the world before birth and before memory was formed, the world of unconscious Thoughts you are naturally and unknowingly using at this very moment. She drew a picture in her journal. It was a picture of a cage that said, "I can't get out". This was accurate. She could not get out and she was dissolving meaning the good in her was giving way to the bad. This is why she called herself "Dissolved Girl".

How deep could the disability be for Sol to call herself a dissolved girl? How bad could the situation be for her, after failing to shoot up a school, to run through the woods and shoot herself in the head with her shotgun?

These could be the words of so many I found in my research.

Symptom 8: They feel they need to remove the disorder to survive.

What I learned from someone with the first prebirth disorder I discovered was that the disability is sometimes very mentally painful and removing it is believed to be needed to survive. For those with that particular disorder, suicide is sometimes the end result.

Testimony from one of the earliest research subjects was priceless. What he said gave me the key to why the people with this disorder felt they had to kill. What I learned from him was that this isn't simply something missing. There was more to the story. Something was driving these people, causing them to use time, energy, money and take tremendous risk to kill others and, if they failed, to kill themselves. Like the man said, "It pops into your head like a sneeze". Now I know what the "it" that pops into your head is.

I knew there was a disorder and I knew I had to figure out what it specifically was. One hint came from the journals of a boy who shot up a High School years ago. He spoke of his "existence" and named his journals such. But it was the words of a young man who committed a mass murder of twelve people in one rampage that gave me the details of the anatomy or the mechanics of Thoughts in the Mind and why it was believed that killing would fulfill the need. This man tried everything he could to stop himself. He went to three psychiatrists, one just before the killing but to no avail because the problem was not in the field of post birth psychology. He also studied neuroscience earning a nearly perfect GPA, but it did not help. It was he who gave me one of the most important clues to why the killing of people who were basically random victims occurred.

The words of the school shooter led me toward understanding somewhat what the missing Thought was, but the words of the mass shooter gave me the specific mechanics of how the person deals with replacing the mental concept that was missing. This man said he went to shoot as many people as possible. That was the whole mission and the alternative was suicide.

62

What he said was completely true. What I learned from him was that this isn't simply something missing, as I had originally thought with the previous subjects. There was more to the story. Something was causing the person to take tremendous risk to kill. Something was driving these people to act in such a damaging way.

Symptom 9: They can feel that the Mind fights back.

One of the most shocking things I learned was that though there is a missing Concept Thought, the Mind fights to use it anyway. From the most benign behavior to the most horrendous behavior, there is the feeling of a drive, a void, sometimes a sucking portal because the Mind fights back. And it does so with a vengeance because that in reality is its job.

I knew the problem was a missing Thought and that it was missing from birth. I had seen it so many times in my students without fully understanding much about it. Mostly, as a teacher, I simply tried to teach them what they could use in place of the missing Thought.

What I didn't know was that the "Task Thought" by the way it was made in "The Natural State of Being" had two parts. Every "Task Thought" in the Mind has two parts. What I didn't realize as well was that the disability caused in the Mind is missing only half of the "Task Thought" that is used to complete tasks. And sometimes the other half fights back.

The Mind, following its programmed instruction in "The Natural State of Being" unbeknownst to the person, tries desperately, to replace the missing part it is trying to use, just like the body tries to heal a cut or wound and replace the missing or damaged cells. It's automatic. It is like a computer that is missing a file, but tries and tries to boot up over and over again. It is no different.

Symptom 10: Relieving the pain from the disorder comes first. Choices about how to do it come second.

If there was a loss of both Concept Thoughts and Action Thoughts in a particular "Task Thought", the person would have no drive, no feeling of loss and no pain. Just as some people rock or run to relieve the feeling, some with prebirth Thought disorders find a solution to the feeling from life, do not do what is illegal, nor do they do what will hurt another person.

The first syndrome I discovered caused people to feel the need to kill another person, which was what got my attention originally. At first, I disregarded a lot of people who killed others from having the first disorder that I discovered because they seemed to have a motive for their actions that had nothing to do with any Prebirth disorder. Maybe they even wrote manifestos saying they wanted to get rid of illegal aliens in the country or prostitutes or whatever. Maybe they said they wanted to get rid of anyone of the gender that hurt them. But it became obvious that something else was wrong. The problem was that, except for choice of victim behavior, they fit all the criteria for having the same first discovered prebirth disorder.

You can liken the choice of who to target to relieve the pain of the Prebirth disorder to going out to eat. The first goal of going out to eat is to relieve the feeling of being hungry. The first goal for these people is to relieve the mental pain from the disorder. Then you choose where you want to go to eat. Maybe you go to an Italian place, maybe Mexican, maybe you go to McDonalds. If you don't really care where you go to eat as long as you eat, that would liken you to one man who had the first discovered prebirth disorder who killed people randomly with no other motive than to kill.

Maybe you go someplace that is easy to get to, a place where you could easily and quickly relieve your hunger. Easily and quickly would be a reason to choose women and children or those who are nearby or those who are easily available. You may choose a place to eat that is familiar, a place that removes your hunger and makes you feel something that has an emotional connection. This would be why someone would kill a person who looks like a relative or former girlfriend. Sometimes there are multiple reasons for victim choice, but the main reason for those who have the first syndrome I discovered is to remove the pain from the disorder that they believe will happen through killing.

Symptom 11: They sometimes collect "Trophies".

Trophies in the forensic world are not trophies as they are not displayed. They are not shown to anyone. They are not set in plain sight for others to see and admire or for the killer to see. They are often hidden in a closet or computer file. Trophies relieve mental pain. They are in fact, in any form, medication. They are there to remind them of what they believed to be the feeling of filling the missing Thought, even for just a small amount of time.

Those with a missing Thought can often relieve the feeling in ways that may be unusual, but not detrimental to others.

Someone with a missing Concept Thought and an active Action Thought who has a missing Thought that deals with intelligence can relieve the pain a little by rocking or running. This gives the person the idea of doing what the Concept Thought should and the Action Thought wants. It is similar to a hamster running on a wheel thinking it is getting somewhere.

Many other syndromes have their own particular ways to fill the missing Thought. Each syndrome requires the Thought it needs to be filled to be done in a different way. Some fulfillment is minor and some is dangerous and hurtful to others depending on the missing Thought.

Symptom 12: They have a lack of remorse.

Those who aren't cognizant of their disorders may do something to hurt another. These are few and far between. They would possibly not realize it, but if told, they would say they were sorry as that is what they were taught. Those of normal or above normal intelligence and cognition who do something to hurt another that has to do with fulfilling the missing Thought would not have remorse. They would feel they need to fill the missing Thought and that taking an action to do so, even though it may hurt another, would not be their fault. It may even be considered God's fault or nature's fault as they feel they were born this way.

Symptom 13: They use defense mechanisms.

Defense mechanisms can be found in the actions of most people whether or not they have a prebirth disorder. They have nothing to do with a prebirth disorder and are not part of the disorder, but are a reaction to being confronted or caught doing something wrong due to the disorder. Some live their lives using defense mechanisms all the time.

Symptom 14: They learn that behavior to remove the pain often doesn't work or doesn't last.

There were very many stories of people who did something to relieve the pain of the loss of a particular Thought only to say it did not work or that it did not last. Some paid heavy prices in their lives to find out the answer to what will remove the pain did not lie in actions they took. Therefore, if the person killed or hurt another to relieve the pain from the lost Thought, they mostly wasted their time and energy.

Symptom 15: They are like this as children.

Yes, it hits the children.

That realization was so hard for me.

It would stand to reason that if this was a disorder from birth, then it would be a disorder of children. So many times, a person will say they knew something was wrong at age five or seven or even earlier. This aspect of things is so sad because it means that there are children walking around with the belief that if they kill or hurt someone, they will feel better. This not only destroys the person because they feel they have to do terrible things to feel better, but it destroys their Equilibrium and sense of morality, causing them to commit crimes since they are already considered by themselves to be bad people.

Symptom 16: They usually have completely innocent parents.

The same family can have a child who does terrible things and another or many others who do not. The family and especially parents of those with a prebirth disorder that causes killing or rape, will often be blamed for things over which they had no control and for which they were not responsible. Often their lives are destroyed by the actions of their loved one. Even if their family member is a simple low functioning person or if they are a high functioning person who does horrendous things the parents pay a high price. Their lives are often never the same, yet they did nothing wrong.

V
Illnesses

CHAPTER 9
Illnesses

Often one will see the same description of the symptoms of a mental disorder because many of those "symptoms" are perfectly normal and part of the person's "Natural State of Being" meaning anyone in their situation of missing Thoughts would act the same way and are correctly reacting to their situation. Being aloof from others if you are unable to understand your own thinking is normal. Being afraid, frustrated, confused when your thinking makes no sense is normal. Being unable to care after a while would be perfectly normal. Being plagued with social anxiety would be normal. Being exhausted after dealing with people would be normal. Being annoyed when someone says they understand and you know they couldn't possibly would be normal. Being sad or depressed over being different from others would be normal. Being someone with few friends would be normal. Many items on the list of symptoms of a particular illness are perfectly normal for a person in that particular circumstance.

Never in my wildest dreams did I think I would have discovered the field of study that held the answer to numerous mental illnesses that psychology cannot explain. Never did it occur to me that my life would go beyond the understanding of the type of special education children with whom I had always worked.

What I have written in this book will take you down a very different path. If you understand it, you will be grateful for it. I thank God for it.

Many of the Thought concepts that make up the Mind of the child were studied in the field called Child Development. These concepts were explained as stages of development in the baby that were learned or appeared after it was born but were not explained as prebirth planted Thoughts though it would make sense some were. The Thoughts were explained but were not distinguished as or considered to be part of a whole as "The Natural State of Being". Though the Thoughts that were in the baby before it was born or that developed later were somewhat understood before my journey began, they had to be dissected and understood with more precision and in more detail especially if the goal is to explain what went wrong.

Everyone who has a disorder that originated before birth, which you will learn about, is also a person. Therefore, along with the disorder they have that originated before birth, they are subject to the disorders that are part of the field of Psychology or things that simply happen in normal life or simple choices they make in life. They are subject to feelings of anger, rage, envy, confusion and all the other maladies that beset human beings along with their disorders.

Multiple Thought disorders.

It is often the case in the world of special education that a student will have multiple issues such as cognitive issues and physical issues or multiple cognitive issues. When discussing disorders that occur in the Prebirth stage of development where multiple Thought elements are not placed before birth as they should be the person could have multiple disorders.

Remember that things can go wrong in both the physical and mental worlds as the child progresses through life as we all know even starting before birth but the plan itself is perfect.

I have discussed how the human is made. "The Natural State of Being" is basically the Grey's Anatomy of the Mind of the human. Along with Grey's Anatomy and the understanding of Psychiatry (Thoughts acquired from living) and Thoughts from before birth, one will have all that needs to be known to understand the basic human being.

How it all started

The first person I tried to understand who had a normal IQ and what I would come to learn to be a prebirth disability was long gone and I was no closer to understanding him when the second person crossed my path. He had many of the same symptoms of the second person except for one major one. The reason for that difference would later become clear. Though I knew little at the time of what was going on, I knew there was an answer for these people but I was far from knowing what it was.

With my students I merely dealt with their disabilities and planned what to teach them to give them the best life possible. I did use research of the professionals to plan their curriculum but never thought to deeply understand the origin of their disabilities and certainly had no thought of healing them. I simply accepted their situation as being the way it was.

The first person destroyed his own life and was basically not a good person in general. He was responsible for hurting others because of choices, greed, selfishness but not because of his disability. His disability basically hurt him but I wanted to know what happened to him anyway.

From my earliest days, I wanted to know what was going on and why people did the things they did. I worked toward understanding and asked for answers to what was going on psychologically with people.

The Innocent Encounter

One fateful day the story of the second person entered my world and I would never be the same. I simply sat to watch a movie and relax before going to sleep not paying much attention to what I was about to see. The movie was about what I thought to be a policeman who abused his badge and killed unsuspecting people he lured into his police car. But I was very wrong.

This was the story of a man who had tremendous power, who was a high-ranking professional military man with a family who stole woman's underwear from houses, raped and killed. His story made no sense as I had always been led to believe that serial killers and rapists did so for power but his man had power beyond belief over women and men. This realization forced me again to want to understand and look deeper.

This man was arrested on rape, murder and other charges. He lost his rank, his home, his freedom for the rest of his life and the military burned his uniforms and any reminder of him.

But why? He didn't need power.

I watched the entire police interview of his arrest. At the very end the detective asked him "If we didn't catch you, would you have done it again?" The man replied, "I was hoping not."

One does not "hope" when one has control. In this situation there was only one reason this type of man would have no control over such behavior. There was only one reason he wouldn't know why he killed and would have had to rely on hope.

I flew off the couch. I paced. "Oh my God. Oh my God". He was one of "ours" meaning he was a special person with what I thought to be a developmental disability. Though I didn't know exactly what the details were, I knew without a doubt he was someone who had a disability which I would find out to be a disability due to the same situation as those who had cognitive disabilities that I had worked with and studied.

When I finally calmed down after rethinking over and over the story of this former soldier and his interrogation the whole thing sunk in and it broke my heart. I knew the incredible tragedy that caused this situation in this man could have been prevented if it was understood. I knew it was nearly the same tragedy that could have been prevented in the person I knew decades before.

I knew that what happened to someone who was in my life decades before was somewhat the same story as what happened to this man who raped and killed and did horrible things. It was the same story of relying on "hope". I knew, though it was a different disorder, the cause was the same.

This time, I was determined to understand completely, and because I now knew more than I knew years before maybe I could do something.

So, I began to study the most extreme situations in order to understand.

I studied serial killers.

I sat in front of my computer day after day, night after night listening to and looking at the most horrific true stories looking for the specific answer to what happened in the case of this former soldier.

I studied him as a person which led to nothing. I found that except for stealing women's underwear, rape and killing he was no different from anyone else. Some people said he was fun and funny. Some said he was extroverted. Some said he was introverted. Many said he was a practical joker. None said he was a possible rapist and serial killer. Not one.

I thought if I could find another who was like him, meaning someone who committed horrible risk-taking crimes with no understanding of why, I could better understand what mentally went wrong with him. Maybe I could understand why he risked everything for what I considered to be nothing.

I did research and more research and got more and more answers. I called those answers revelations because they revealed to me what was needed to take the next step toward my understanding and discovery of the field of what I call Epistemic Psychology and the disorders that had their origin in the stage of development before birth.

I studied this second person whose story entered my life and who had what seemed a normal IQ or possibly high IQ and what I believe to be a prebirth disorder. And who happened to be a serial killer. The third and fourth people I learned about were researched because they were killers as well and seemed to have the same disorder and use the same words when caught.

The third subject I studied was seventeen years old. He was labeled having a disorder from the Schizophrenia Spectrum which tends to be the go-to diagnosis though there were never any psychotic signs. This was to me completely ridiculous and I found that psychiatrists would adjust the psychological requirements and descriptions to fit the disorder. A sad thing.

The fourth subject was a brilliant young man who went to three psychiatrists to get help and studied neuroscience to help himself. He was unable to control his behavior and committed a mass murder.

All four subjects had their lives destroyed as well as destroying other lives that touched theirs.

The more I studied the more I found. And all had the same general symptoms as so many other killers or serial killers.

These are the names of some who I believe had the same disorder as subjects two, three and four and many others I studied. James, William, Dennis, Austin, Dayton, David, Daniel, Dylan, Ted, Phillip, F.W., Gary, Evan, Ed, another Ed, Jeffrey, Ted, Monte, Mark, Belle, Alyssa, Noah, Wayne, Wesley, another James, Henry, Ricardo, Juan, Andrei, another William, Stephan, Samuel, another David, Gerard, Charles, George, Karl, Sol, Matthew, Bruce, Robert, Elizabeth, Scott, Israel just to name a few. In reality, I had pages and pages of names of people with the same symptoms and what I would call a syndrome.

The general symptoms I found with people who have a prebirth disorder are as follows:

1. They are driven to behave in a way they do not want. Often a person with a particular before birth syndrome will ask for help, study a related field to understand to not behave as they are prone to do or even take steps that will damage or end their life.
2. They have no control over their behavior no matter how detrimental it is. As I studied people with Prebirth syndromes it was repeatedly stated that they cannot control their Thoughts. This stands to reason since they had no idea why they were so driven and the disorder is all they know.

3. They have no idea why they behave as they do. Those with the highest intelligence will say when asked why that smarter men then they could not figure it out or their psychologists will say "he has no idea why he did the things he did" which is true due to the disorder beginning before memory is formed.

4. They are completely misunderstood or ununderstood by all who are a party to the disorder. The labels placed on those who have Prebirth disabilities are often simply labels and the misrepresentation of the things said by those with Prebirth disorders is shocking as the professionals try to make sense of what they do not understand.

5. The desire to fix the disability comes on quickly (like a sneeze) and causes a behavior. Due to the type of disorder the need to use what is not there comes on quickly like someone who keeps forgetting he is missing the bottom of his leg but without thinking, tries to walk.

6. They tend to bounce from theory to theory to find the answer to their disability. In their desperate attempt to understand and explain their actions many will go from one cause to another and back again then contradict the original theory because they don't really know why.

7. They feel they live in another dimension or the other side of the window from other people.

8. There is a tremendous overwhelming drive to fulfill a need to stop the feeling from the disorder. This drive often fills the void left from the missing Thought in the syndrome but it often does not work or works only temporarily because it is believed it would.

9. There is a constant unconscious fight going on in the Mind as it fights back to fix the disorder. As you will see the way the Mind is made will cause it to fight back to replace what is missing just as a cut on your hand fights to replace the damaged or missing cells.

10. The drive to relieve the feeling from the disorder comes first. Often people will say the person with the Prebirth disorder is doing a particular thing for revenge or anger and so on but the desire to relieve pain from the damage from the syndrome is the ultimate goal.

11. They often are desperate for any reminder of behavior that relieved the pain. Because they think a particular behavior will fix the problem, they will often try to get that temporary relief to stop the pain for just a moment.

12. They do not feel responsible for their actions as they were born with the need to take them. This is stated over and over in their words and actions when confronted with their behavior.

13. They will often do things as a defense mechanism which are mistakenly connected to the disorder. A defense mechanism is in the Psychology realm and is natural and not part of a Prebirth disability.

14. As time goes on, they realize that things they tried to relieve the pain do not work or only work temporarily and since they have no other solution for relief, they may take their lives.

15. It hits the children though they don't realize it. Many will say they were born with something wrong and that they knew something was wrong or missing as early as age five. They are correct. This throws their equilibrium off from the very beginning as they are left alone to cope with the Thought that they are bad people for their Thoughts.

16. Some become bitter and behave with cruelty later in life out of anger and revenge.

17. Many look like any other person and behave normally most of the time.

18. Most come from good loving families who have no idea where the disorder came from.

The disabilities that happened before birth were all similar because they were caused by the same basic situation yet they were also different because the individual Thought that was missing was different. I was beginning to learn about Prebirth Psychology and didn't know any details about any of it. I especially didn't know its components.

The general mental cause of disabilities that happen is the same but the specifics are different for each disability or what I would call syndrome. For example, Bennett Syndrome, Corpal Syndrome and Astore Syndrome are each caused by the loss of a Thought that was not properly placed before birth. But the missing Thoughts for each syndrome were particular Thoughts causing particular needs to be filled and particular behaviors. The absence of each particular Thought would cause a different set of needs, a different set of behaviors and a different syndrome.

It was the lack of logic that prompted me to look further and judge the accuracy of the most commonly accepted beliefs for the reason for the behavior of the soldier turned rapist/ killer.

It was the disability of the former soldier I focused on in my earliest studies not knowing there would be so many with similar symptoms, not knowing the origin of the disability, and certainly not knowing anything about a Prebirth disability, its components or its existence.

It was time to dive to the deepest part of the psyche and uncover what was really happening.

A note on culpability: When the behavior of the person is considered to be a mental disorder, the disorder will most often be due to something that happened before birth and/or before memory was formed. For some a disorder prior to the formation of consciously retrievable memory effects the post memory Thoughts concerning choice but this is very rare. Choice is often logical and seldom is completely influenced by the loss from Thoughts not planted in the unborn baby. If there is cognition that allows the person to have a conscience or to understand the law then the person must obey the law and their conscience. Having a Prebirth disorder does not excuse behavior especially illegal behavior unless cognition is so severely damaged as to keep the person from knowing right from wrong.

CHAPTER 10
A syndrome

Just today, years after starting to write this book, I came across a syndrome that the author said explained serial killing. I wondered if all my research could be wrong? Could it be that someone else had a different explanation that was researched, tested and proven? Again, and hopefully for the last time, I researched this syndrome and it was simply a list of symptoms with no explanation of why or what to do.

Injury to the unborn baby that happened between conception and 20 weeks of gestation, blocks a Thought that was to be placed in the Mind, causing eventual mental injury in the child or adult. At the stage before memory is formed Thoughts are systematically placed in the Mind of the unborn child either as a single Thought or in a specific series of Thoughts to be used after birth and throughout the life of the being. These millions or billions of Thoughts called "Task Thoughts" allow the child to perform a particular task and each thought performs its task over and over throughout its life.

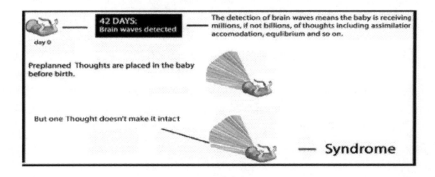

When one specific Thought is not placed intact in the unborn child's Mind, a disorder will occur. A Syndrome is caused, by the missing "Task Thought", by the missing Concept Thought part of the "Task Thought" or a missing Action Thought part of the "Task Thought".

At this time, we are mostly working on the situation of a missing Concept and an active Action Thought as the cause of syndromes. The person with this disorder would have Thoughts which, if understood, would logically though incorrectly, lead to the conclusion that a particular action will relieve the pain. This incorrect Thought in some disorders have caused school shootings, serial killings, random killings, mass murders and suicides.

Bennett Syndrome was the first disorder that began before the baby was born to be discovered.

The progression went from

- o questioning why a particular man did what he did
- o to understanding he had a prebirth disorder
- o to realizing so many others had this disorder as well.
- o to realizing the Thought had components.
- o to realizing what the components were.
- o to realizing there was a missing Thought.
- o to realizing there was a desire to fill the missing part
- o to realizing there was a powerful drive toward fulfillment
- o to applying "The Natural State of Being"
- o to dissecting Thoughts
- o to understanding before birth disorders
- o to understanding the disorder of Bennett Syndrome
- o to realizing that Bennett Syndrome was not the only disorder that began before the child was born.

The number of syndromes that can be caused by a missing Thought that was not placed properly before birth is enormous. Some cause major issues for the person, but most just cause little idiosyncrasies and are funny or an annoyance. For instance, I have a spatial issue. My friend's sideways driveway was impossible for me as is hanging a picture on the wall that someone doesn't eventually come along and straighten.

The Thoughts placed in us as the program I call "The Natural State of Being" are too numerous to discuss here as are their counterpart syndromes. Discovering all the syndromes that are important enough to cause major issues that begin before birth will take research and time. The ones understood at this time are included in this book.

In addition to syndromes that began in the Prebirth stage, there are disorders that are caused by the action of "The Natural State of Being" and its impact on post memory Thoughts as well as simple choice. I will explain in detail Prebirth Syndromes and the Thoughts that are missing if that information is available. At some point, I will also discuss disorders that are prebirth that have a Thought added to them, post memory Thoughts and choices. All have a connection to "The Natural State of Being".

The three kinds of Thoughts:

One more very important thing that has to be understood is that there are three kinds of Thoughts. The three kinds of individual Thoughts are the Thoughts that have to do with Life, the Thoughts that have to do with Truth and the Thoughts that have to do with Love.

The Life kind of Thoughts would include Thoughts, like the being's place in the world or the being's concept of being a human or personality and talents. The Truth kind of Thoughts would include the facts or Truths that we use to live. The concept of Assimilation, Accommodation and one type of Equilibrium would be this kind of Thought, as well as other factual unemotional concepts.

The Love kind of Thought would be basically self-explanatory. The happiness a baby has when it achieves something or when you make a funny face at it comes from a Thought planted from "The Natural State of Being". Two Prebirth Thoughts of the Love kind that are currently known are the Love of self and the Love of others.

Reception and expression of each kind of Thought.

All three kinds of Thoughts when used are either received or expressed.

One can receive all the Love in the world but if it isn't expressed there is a disorder. Receiving and expressing Love is very different. A person can do something horrendously wrong and still be loved by family and even admit to being loved or a person can Love themselves or others though they were horribly mistreated as a child.

One who teaches anything is expressing Truth and on the same note one who learns is receiving Truth.

A person who simply regurgitates answers with no input from their personality will be expressing Truth but will not be expressing Life. I know an anesthesiologist who is like that and, though good at his job, he merely spits out facts and repeats actions he was taught in school. Anything out of the norm would throw him off. He may enjoy (receive) the things of Life like music but you will never see him create anything. And he certainly couldn't create something abstract that doesn't use the rules that are the norm.

Each kind of Thought is on its own. There are Concept Thoughts of the kind dealing with Life, Concept Thoughts of the kind dealing with Truth and Concept Thoughts of the kind dealing with Love. All Thoughts no matter the kind are separate, but work together for the being to live and grow. Future research will undoubtedly produce more Thoughts of each kind but there are only three kinds of Thoughts.

The power of Equilibrium.

The Concept of Equilibrium can be found in two kinds of Thoughts. One kind of Thought is Truth as when it is part of the series that includes Assimilation and Accommodation. Another kind of Thought is Love as when a person believes things should be right meaning fair and equal. The same Concept of Equilibrium is in use but is different. One concept is used as a part of Truth and the other concept is used as part of Love meaning the world should be fair.

The power of fear.

Research for this book was done using the testimonies of those with the disorders in conjunction with Jean Piaget, a man I trust implicitly and who simply, in my opinion, researched and reported in his own words what already existed as "The Natural State of Being".

A word must be said for the huge role, of what those who deal with physical disorders call the Cytokine Storm. It has been said that the reason the Covid-19 virus caused mild cases in most and was fatal for others was due to the Cytokine Storm. In many cases it seemed that the worst damage may have been driven by the deranged immune response to the infection, rather than the virus itself. In many of the sickest patients with Covid-19, their blood was teeming with high levels of immune system proteins called Cytokines. Scientists believe these cytokines are evidence of the immune response called the cytokine storm, where the body starts to attack its own cells and tissues rather than just fighting off the virus. One study of patients who died of H1N1 influenza found that 81% had features of cytokine storm. What happens is that many cells that are infected send out an SOS as a protective mechanism. In Covid-19 Dr. Kumar said, "Basically, most of your cells die because of the cytokine storm. It eats away at the lung. They cannot recover. It seems to play a role in death in a large number of cases".

So why am I telling you this? I believe the Mind does the same. As the Mind perceives a threat or is faced with what it does not understand, it basically… panics. This fear of what is pending or happening can prevent healing.

I believe that once a person understands, even in a severe illness like Bennett Syndrome, the fear will stop and the healing will begin. Once Truth and understanding enters, the fear… the cytokine storm… will be replaced with healing.

It needs to be said that it is not unusual for a serial killer, rapist or killer to have an extremely high IQ. The normal IQ for most people is 100. The following killers/rapists are listed with their IQs. Nathan Leopold 210, Richard Loeb 160, Ted Kaczynski 167, Charlene Williams 160, Kristin Gilbert 152, Andrew Cunanan 147, Jeffrey Dahmer 115, Harold Shipman 140, Rodney Alcala 135, Ed Kemper 129, Joel Rifkin 129, Gary Ridgway 118, Ed Gein 106, Ken Bianchi 116. This situation happens, I believe, because the unborn baby suffers a quick lack of oxygen which sends the child's Mind into turmoil and disequilibrium and a cytokine storm causing the Action Thought to overreact out of fear. As anyone knows if there is fear the body goes into overdrive. It runs, shakes, yells, screams, it overthinks and so on. In this instance this overdrive causes a surge in energy linked to the intellect. Some will cause a surge in other areas. Some will cause a surge in action leaving the child in a hyperactive state.

CHAPTER 11
The First Syndrome Discovered

This book was written basically in chronological order as I learned what was going on. The first disorder I discovered and understood was connected to the killer that I first studied. I named this disorder a syndrome because by definition it is a syndrome.

BENNETT SYNDROME

Prebirth Thought: The concept of Life (single Thought)

Prebirth injury: Loss of Concept Thought, overactive or intact Action Thought

Reaction to injury: Drive to replace the missing Thought with the life of another

Kind of Thought: Life

Street Name/Psychology Name: none

Special Note: The Thoughts that are missing in Bennett Syndrome are in no way connected to the Thoughts of conscience or the intellectual understanding of the law or of rules.

"Mom, I'm a monster."

Bennett Syndrome is a mental disorder that began in the unborn baby between conception and the time when the baby is able to sustain itself as a viable life form.   Bennett Syndrome is a unique disorder that can cause severe mental pain, disequilibrium and depression from which the sufferer desperately tries to get relief.

Here damage to the unborn baby blocks a Thought from being placed. In this case, it was the Concept Thought that was not placed in the mind. This loss causes mental pain as the Action Thought is intact. This takes place in the life category of Thought types which logically, though incorrectly, leads the sufferer to the conclusion that killing will relieve the pain and return the "life" concept to the person's psyche. The desire to get relief from this disorder has caused school shootings, serial killing, mass murders and suicides.

Before memory is formed Thoughts are systematically placed in the Mind of the unborn child in a specific pattern to be used after birth.   These millions or billions of Thoughts called "Task

Thoughts" each allows the child to perform a particular task and each performs its task over and over throughout the child's life.

When one specific Thought is not placed intact or at all in the unborn child's Mind due to what is currently considered medically uncorroborated circumstances a disorder will occur.

Bennett Syndrome is one of the disorders caused, not by the missing "Task Thought", but by the missing Concept part of the "Task Thought". This leaves the Action Thought part of the "Task Thought" to fight for its survival and create the overwhelming drive to complete the task. It is that drive that causes the belief in the need to kill.

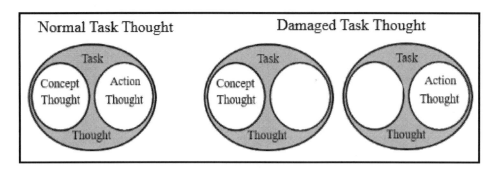

Because Bennett Syndrome is a disorder that begins before birth it is as deep and infiltrating as it could possibly be.

Bennett Syndrome causes:

- Severe mental pain:

  "I feel like a pot of scolding (sic) water on the verge of boiling over... so dangerously close to spilling over. and what that may cause is yet to be seen and most likely a hazard, to myself and others. I'm afraid of my currently unknown capacity for pain and misery and anger. Each time it gets exponentially worse and worse. my soul is in deep suffering and dis-belonging. I have done quite a good job at keeping all of the explosive energy inside of me but every time... worse and worse and worse." – Sol Pais shot herself in the head after failing to shoot up Denver schools*

- Lack of control over the Thought:
  "Please catch me...I cannot control myself" – Lipstick killer, William Heirens

- The Thought that killing will relieve the pain:
  "Shootings were supposed to increase my self-worth and get me out of the depression. If you take lives away it sort of adds to your own value. What they would have done gets canceled and goes to me. No logic. It's just the way it is." – young man/mass murderer

-
-
-

- Behavior with no understanding of the cause:

"I don't know why it started. I don't have any definite answers on that myself. If I knew the true, real reasons why all this started, before it ever did, I wouldn't probably have done any of it." Jeffrey Dahmer, serial killer

One characteristic of Bennett Syndrome is that the person behaves in a way that they cannot themselves explain. This behavior is often destructive to the person and others. When asked why they behave as they do, referring to killing, the person with Bennett Syndrome will truthfully answer that they have no idea. This is because there was no memory from before the disorder happened as memory of the missing Thought had not been formed.

Studies have been done for decades on those who behave according to the symptoms of Bennett Syndrome revealing little if anything. This is due to the fact that the people studying this did not know of "The Natural State of Being" or the possibility of a missing Concept Thought.

Bennett Syndrome does not affect learning in any way. Those with Bennett Syndrome can have anywhere from low IQ levels to extremely high IQ levels and can be found in higher economic or status positions. Bennett Syndrome does not affect the understanding of rules and laws.

Bennett Syndrome is a disorder where the sufferer lives a normal and often productive life between outbreaks. When the outbreaks occur, they hit hard and the sufferer behaves in an extremely bizarre and often dangerous manner. This, normal until horrendously bizarre, situation causes those around the sufferer to say they had no clue the person would do the things they did and often be in denial of such behavior. It is also the reason serial killer Ted Bundy said he was ninety nine percent normal and one percent killer.

Those with Bennett Syndrome feel a loss that is debilitating when it hits and take action in order to relieve the pain in ways they cannot explain.

There are at times other Prebirth disorders that accompany Bennett Syndrome causing the sufferer to do even more unrelated and bizarre things.

Often those who suffer with Bennett Syndrome will have additional issues in the field of Psychology and use such things as what Freud called defense mechanisms. Prejudice can be present as well as revenge and blame. Confusion and lack of understanding will cause the person to repeatedly express differing reasons for their behavior which is common since the person has no clue why it all was happening and is trying to find out as well.

Indications of Bennett Syndrome

Extreme, feeling of loss at a very early age with no opposing memory for comparison.

Awareness of the loss and a feeling of being very different from other human beings.

Awareness that others do not have the loss.

Psychological behaviors from the feeling of loss such as anger, revenge, jealousy, blame.

Extreme desire to fill the loss to the point of endangering themselves and/or others.

Depression to point of suicide or killing.

The logical conclusion in some, due to the nature of the disorder, that to take life from another will fill the loss.

The actions of alcoholism, drug use, suicide, serial killing, mass murder.

Possible killing of animals at an early age to relieve the pain and to avoid killing humans.

Basic random killing.

Other indications of Bennett Syndrome

Obsession with death

The study of psychology, neuroscience, other psychological fields and sometimes medical science toward healing then studying criminology when the previous studies produced no healing fruit.

Irritability

Acting out at a young age.

Bennett Syndrome Progression

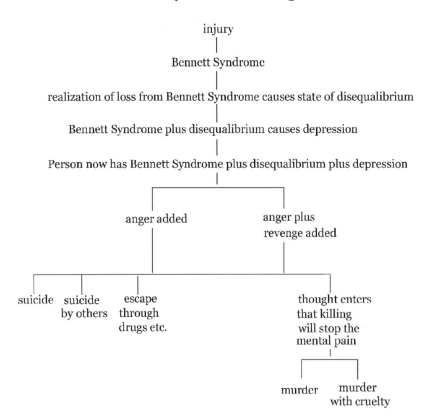

Statements of those who killed and showed symptoms of Bennett Syndrome

Ricardo Caputo, serial killer: "I turned myself in in order to avoid more killings. When I did what I did I was sick and I hope that I can be cured while I am incarcerated. That's all I have to say."

William Heirens, serial killer: "For heaven's sake catch me before I kill more. I cannot control myself"

Mark Conditt, Austin bomber stated he had always been a psychopath.

Sean Gillis when asked about himself. "The word monster come to mind."

H.H. Holmes, America's first recorded serial killer: "I could not help the fact that I was a murderer, no more than the poet can help the inspiration to sing. I was born with the evil one standing as my sponsor beside my bed where I was ushered into the world and he has been with me since."

Ted Bundy after being asked why: "That's the question of the hour isn't it? And one that people much more intelligent than I have been working on for years, one that I've been working on for years and trying to understand."

Jeffrey Dahmer, serial killer, his testimony at trial: "I wanted to find out just what it was that caused me to be so bad and evil but most of all, Mr. Boyle (attorney) and I decided that maybe there was a way for us to tell the world that if there are people out there with these disorders, maybe they can get some help before they end up being hurt or hurting someone...". "I don't know why it started. I don't have any definite answers on that myself. If I knew the true, real reasons why all this started, before it ever did, I wouldn't probably have done any of it."

Jeffrey Dahmer on serial killing: "It didn't satisfy me completely so maybe I was thinking another one will".

Bennett Syndrome is a severe mental disorder where the sufferers will often kill themselves or others to relieve the pain. If they kill, they will kill randomly but will often have a preference of who to kill that is secondary to the killing. They may choose one who looks like someone as a type of revenge or children, women or those in close proximity because that is easiest, those with whom they are annoyed such as immigrants, Jews, whites, blacks and so on. These are secondary as the killing always comes first.

Bennett Syndrome seems to be extremely prevalent in particular geographical areas like Denver and the possible cause of a high rate of teenage suicides in High Schools, high rate of school shootings and mass murders and in Vail Colorado the highest suicide rate in the country. This suggests that research into causation should take place in such geographical areas.

History of Revelations that lead to the discovery of Bennett Syndrome

Bennett Syndrome was the first disorder I discovered. This discovery came about by studying a particular criminal. This is the list of revelations that led to the discovery of "The Natural State of Being", Action/Concept Thoughts, missing Thoughts and various Syndromes.

Some of the names and details concerning the people were changed.

Revelations 1: The first thing I learned was that a man I will call R.W., second in command at a high-ranking military base who had a wife and a good life didn't want to kill. That was quite a shocking thing to learn as I always Thought killers were happy with killing.

Revelation 2: The second thing I learned was that R.W. had no control to stop no matter what the cost.

At some point I knew R.W. had a disability but I Thought it was mostly just him at first. It was obvious from the words of R.W. that he had no control. But what about others? The more I studied, the more I found.

I want you to meet William Heirens. The year was 1945. He was 17 years old.

These are his loving parents who came to see him after he tried to kill himself. As you will learn there were many loving parents in these stories.

William wrote this note in lipstick on the wall above his victim causing him to be called The Lipstick Killer. What it basically said was what was said in other terms by R.W. which was that he can't stop. Once caught this 17-year-old boy will spend the rest of his life in prison and die there.

This is Ricardo Caputo on the left. He said, "I turned myself in in order to avoid more killings. When I did what I did I was sick and I hope that I can be cured while I am incarcerated." He too, would die in prison having never been cured.

My studies took me not only back in time but to very faraway places though I didn't have to go far to find serial killers and killers with the disorder. They were everywhere. All over our country. All over other countries.

Stephen Akinmurele, London England, is on the top right. He said, "I can't help the way I feel, what I did was wrong. I know that and I feel for them but it doesn't mean I won't do it again."

This was said by H.H. Holmes, bottom right. The year is 1861. "I could not help the fact that I was a murderer, no more than the poet can help the inspiration to sing. I was born with the evil one standing as my sponsor beside my bed where I was ushered into the world and he has been with me since."- Notice the dated picture. I have found people with this disorder back centuries.

This was said by another man: "When this monster entered my brain, I will never know, but it's here to stay. How does one cure himself? I can't stop it, the monster goes on, and hurts me as well as society. Maybe you can stop it. I can't."

Jeffrey Dahmer had his own words for it.

Revelation 3: The third thing I learned was that R.W. had a disability that was before birth causing him not only to have no control over his action to kill but no knowledge of why he killed. When serial killer Ted Bundy was asked why he killed he said, "smarter men than me have tried to figure that out."

Revelation 4: In all the years I watched criminal shows and in all the articles I read or stories I heard concerning serial killers I was always told they did what they did for control. I was led to believe they wanted to overpower their victims and that was their sole reason for killing. But R.W. had all the control one could want so that was not true. So, the fourth thing I learned which was revelation four was that the FBI and the police have the motive for serial killing completely wrong.

The number of serial killers who had the same disorder as R.W., especially the lack of ability to stop, was staggering. Instead of a few, I found hundreds who basically said, "I was hoping not" and I know I could have found thousands if I looked longer.

Learning More Details

I had the general concept of what happened concerning R.W. just as I had a general concept of what happened concerning my students but I needed something more specific.

My students simply lived their lives and often did so happily so I never felt compelled to dig any deeper than I already had for them. But in the cases of people like R.W. people were dying and they were dying horrible deaths. I had to understand more.

Knowing very little about serial killers at all except what I had seen on television shows I was confused about what actually happened to R.W.. This man had everything. He had control and he had the means to do what is very masculine. He flew airplanes. He wore a uniform. He was in charge of hundreds of people.

I was curious, if you disregard the rape and killing, about why, if he wanted to dress in woman's underwear, he didn't simply buy underwear from Sears to wear instead of stealing them from neighbors and risking everything to do so.

The whole thing didn't fit.

Revelation 6: They have no idea why.

As I studied and listened to only the words of serial killers ignoring the opinions of reporters, police, psychiatrists and such, I found the killers themselves were searching for the reasons they killed. Often, they would jump from this reason to that reason and back again.

These are the words of Jeffrey Dahmer. a man who killed seventeen men and boys and ate some of his victims, at his sentencing. "Your Honor, it is over now. It has never been a case of wanting to get free. I didn't ever want freedom, Frankly, I wanted death for myself. This was a case to tell the world that I did what I did not for reasons of hate. I hated no one. I know I was sick or evil or both. Now I believe I was sick. The doctors have told me about my sickness and now I have some peace. I know how much harm I have caused. I tried to do the best I could after the arrest to make amends but no matter what I did I could not undo the terrible harm I have caused. I feel so bad for what I did to those poor families and I understand their rightful hate. I decided to go through with this trial for a number of reasons. One reason was to let the world know these were not hate crimes. I wanted the world of Milwaukee which I deeply hurt to know the truth of what I did. I didn't want unanswered questions. All the questions have been answered. I wanted to find out just what it was that caused me to be so bad and evil but most of all Mr. Boyle and I decided that maybe there was a way for us to tell the world that if there are people out there with these disorders maybe they can get some help before they end up being hurt or hurting someone. I think the trial did that".

Thomas Dillon on the killing of a young man. "Paxton was killed because of an irresistible compulsion that has taken over my life. I knew when I left my house that day that someone would die by my hand. I just didn't know who or where. I'm an average looking person with a family, a job, a home just like yourself. Something in my head causes me to turn into a merciless killer with no conscience".

Revelation 7: They live in another Dimension

The depth of this disorder is one that is very hard to explain. When this particular disorder hits, which is about 1% of the person's day, it is all-encompassing. It is like the intense darkness when there is no light available at all.

The movie Sybil does a great job unveiling the dark depths of things in this dimension. I believe everyone who reads this book should watch the movie "Sybil" as it truly shows the depth of these disorders. For your information Sybil and Dr. Wilbur were like mother and daughter the rest of their lives and Sybil said it happened just as the book stated.

Sol Pais was still a teenager when she attempted to shoot up schools in Denver. When she failed, she ran through the woods with her pump action shotgun and shot herself in the head which killed her instantly. The reporters said her writing was filled with angst. That must have been some angst. In her angst filled journals she said, "I live in another dimension".

The thing is that Sol really did live in another dimension. I am going to take you through that dimension. The dimension of most serial killers, mass murderers, random killers and some suicides.

This is a journey through another dimension, one that began in the Mind of the killer before memory was formed. Welcome to the understanding of what makes a killer kill. And welcome to the world of prebirth disorders that can explain the thinking of so many who cannot be helped with typical psychology and cannot help themselves without this information.

The depth and loneliness of this disorder is all the sufferers know. The loss from this disorder is all encompassing. The emptiness is powerful and comes on with a force. and sometimes very quickly.

This is Sol Pais. She was able to explain what it was like to have this disorder from a female's very creative point of view. I learned of the depth of this syndrome from her. She called the world she lived in another dimension. And it was another dimension because it was so hidden and it was a place her Mind unconsciously went to all the time.

It was the dimension of someone continually being tossed into a world where there is no understanding and where no one else exists. It was the dimension of where the missing Thought was. One serial killer called it the other side of the window. Jeffrey Dahmer said he knew something was missing and said, "I felt so completely different having to live in a world of people who were not like me". Another man said somewhat accurately he was two different people.

The reason it was another dimension is because it deals with the world before memory was formed, the world of unconscious Thoughts you are naturally and unknowingly using at this very moment.

But Sol wasn't the only one. Why did she fly to Denver to shoot up schools there? Because that was where another person was who she could relate to because he had the same disorder. She called him Dyl in her journals.

A picture in her journal was a drawn picture of a cage that said, "I can't get out". This was accurate. She could not get out and she was dissolving meaning the good in her was giving way to the bad. This is why she called herself "Dissolved Girl".

How deep could the disability be for her to call herself dissolved girl? How bad could the situation be for her after failing to shoot up a school to run through the woods and shoot herself in the head with her shotgun?

These are her words, "I feel like a pot of scolding (sic) water on the verge of boiling over… so dangerously close to spilling over… and what that may cause is yet to be seen and most likely a hazard, to myself and others. I'm afraid of my currently unknown capacity for pain and misery and anger. Each time it gets exponentially worse and worse. My soul is in deep suffering and dis-belonging. I have done quite a good job at keeping all of the explosive energy inside of me but every time… worse and worse and worse."

These could be the words of so many I found in my research.

Revelation 8: They feel they need to kill to survive

What I learned from the testimony of a man I will call J.H. who killed many in one mass murder spree was priceless. What he said gave me the key to why the people with this disorder had to kill. What I learned from him was that this isn't simply something missing. There was more to the story. Something was driving these people causing them to use time, energy, money and take tremendous risk to kill.

I knew there was something mentally wrong and I knew I had to figure out what it specifically was.

But it was the words of J.H. who shot up a large room of people that gave me the details of the anatomy or the mechanics or what Jean Piaget called the genetic epistemology of Thoughts in the Mind and why killing would fulfill the need. He tried everything he could to stop himself. He went to three psychiatrists, one just before the killing but to no avail. He also studied in the Psychological field getting a 3.969 GPA; but it did not help. It was he who gave me one of the most important clues to why the killing of people who were basically random victims occurred.

He said that his whole mission was to kill so that what the person did in their life went to him with the alternative being suicide.

What J.H. said was completely true and what I learned from him was that this isn't simply something missing as I had originally Thought with R.W.. There was more to the story. Something was causing the person to use time, energy, money and take tremendous risk to kill. Something was driving these people to act in such a self and non-self-damaging way.

Revelation 9: The Mind fights back.

The most horrendous behavior of killers who have the same disorder as R.W., J.H. and so on comes because the Mind fights back. I will explain this in detail later in this book.

I knew the problem was a missing Thought and that it was missing from birth. I had seen it so many times in my students without fully understanding it. Mostly as a teacher I simply tried to teach them what they could use in place of the missing Thought.

What I didn't know was that the "Task Thought" by the way it was made in "the Natural State of Being" had two parts. As you will learn every "Task Thought" in the Mind has two parts. What I didn't realize was that the disability in killers is missing only half of the "Task Thought" that is in the Mind that is used to complete tasks.

Therefore, the Mind following its programmed instruction in "The Natural State of Being" unbeknownst to the person tries desperately and with a vengeance to replace the missing part it is trying to use just like the body tries to heal a cut or wound and replace the missing or damaged cells. It's automatic like the computer with the missing of a file. It is no different.

Many killers keep journals before they kill. The young boy who shot up the High School wrote in his journal about his existence and named his journal such. The missing half of the Task Thought that deals with a life component had to be replaced with the "existence" of another as you already heard a killer say.

Revelation 10: The killing comes first. The choice of who to kill comes second.

At first, I disregarded a lot of school shooters and mass murderers and so on because they seemed to have a motive that had nothing to do with the killing disorder. Maybe they even left manifestos saying they wanted to get rid of illegal aliens in the country or people they didn't like or prostitutes or whatever. Maybe they said they wanted to get rid of anyone of the gender that hurt them. But it became obvious that there was a problem. The problem was that except for choice of victim behavior, they fit all the criteria for having this disorder.

You can liken the choice of who to kill to going out to eat. The first goal is to eat to relieve the feeling of being hungry. The first goal for the killer is to relieve mental pain by killing.

Then you choose where you want to go to eat. Maybe you go to an Italian place, maybe Mexican, maybe you go to McDonalds. If you don't really care where you go to eat as long as you eat that would liken you to a killer like the one named David who killed randomly with no other motive but to kill.

Maybe you go someplace that is easy to get to, a place where you could easily and quickly relieve your hunger. Easily and quickly would be a reason to choose women and children or those who are nearby or those who are easily available. A good example of that would be the Santa Rosa hitchhiker killer or the Craigslist killer, Philip Markoff.

In addition, you may choose a place to eat that is familiar, a place that removes your hunger and makes you feel something that has an emotional connection. That would be the choices made by Ted Bundy whose emotional connection was revenge or Jeffrey Dahmer whose emotional connection had to do with young men which is another syndrome.

Sometimes there are multiple reasons for victim choice but the main reason for those with Bennett Syndrome is to kill.

Revelation 11: Trophies: Trophies in the forensic world are not trophies as they are not displayed. They are not shown to anyone. They are not set in plain sight for purposes of ego for others to see or for the killer to see. They are often hidden in a closet or computer file.

Trophies relieve mental pain. Though serial killers will say that the killing doesn't work it brings temporary satisfaction in the belief that it will relieve the pain. That temporary belief feels good which is why they kill again and again. It is also why they need to be reminded of the feeling.

Trophies can be so many things. But what they really are is the reliving of the killing so the pain will be relieved and it is at almost any cost.

Ted Bundy did two things to seal his fate toward execution in the electric chair. First when he escaped, he immediately killed again. Instead of simply enjoying his newfound freedom he killed. It seems a bit stupid for a person who was just handed some freedom to immediately risk losing it.

Second was that at his trial he was his own attorney and as such he could question people on the stand. Blinded by his desperate need to relive the situation he called the detective in his case to the stand and asked the detective right in the middle of his trial in front of the jury to explain in detail the crime scene. This sealed his fate to the jury and he was found guilty and executed by electric chair.

So again, why did he do that? He did it because crime scenes, trophies, trinkets, pictures, heads in a refrigerator, strangling a person and returning them to life to strangle them again and so on are in fact, medication. They bring the person back to the feeling of fulfilling the missing Thought.

Revelation 12: Remorse: Killers often don't feel remorse because they feel they were born this way and not responsible. Many will cry over the pain the families are going through but seldom over the pain for the victim.

Killer William Bonin said, "I couldn't help myself. It's not my fault I killed them boys".

Revelation 13: Defense mechanisms: A school shooter from Illinois wrote the word "killer" in big letters on the front of his tee-shirt which he displayed to the court at sentencing. One pedophile killer attacked the father of his victim in court. These behaviors are from the psychology field and are best explained to be one of Freud's defense mechanisms.

Revelation 14: It doesn't work. It doesn't last. Paul, after shooting up the room in prison made the statement, "it didn't work". A killer from the 1970s said, "I was literally singing to myself on the way home after the killing. The tension, the desire to kill a woman had built up in such explosive proportions that when I finally pulled the trigger, all the pressures, all the tensions, all the hatred had just vanished, dissipated, but only for a short time.

Revelation 15: It hits the children

It would stand to reason that if this was a disorder from birth that it would be a disorder of children.

Pictured: Jeffrey Dahmer top left, Ted Bundy middle, Wesley Todd bottom right.

It hits the children. One man who killed numerous men said he knew something was missing when he was seven-years-old. Since this began before birth such a statement would make perfect sense. I heard the recording of him saying this and I groaned causing someone to ask me if I was ok. I said "yes" but I was not ok.

At that moment, I realized that there were children who though they had happiness in their lives in other ways and enjoyed often wonderful families and experiences were walking around with this disorder thinking they are monsters inside, carrying the horrendous burden of feeling they need to kill and doing so all alone.

This is Mark Conditt, Austin Texas serial bomber: "I am a psychopath, have always been one. I wish I were sorry, but I am not".

I had often read when studying serial killers that they had always been psychopaths. But here is the thing…a psychopath has no empathy, no remorse, no attachments and so on but this person spent his time and money planning to kill. A psychopath wouldn't care if he/she killed. Killers like Arthur Shawcross are psychopathic killers killing because someone took their parking spot or he thought they stole from him. But one with this disorder would purposely kill for no seemingly logical reason and risk so much to do so. So, I believe Mark Conditt also had the disorder that I found that I call Bennett Syndrome.

 Another man who stated he was like this from birth was Andrei Chikatilo, Soviet Union serial killer who said: "I know I have to be destroyed. I was a mistake of nature".

At age 10-11 a little girl from England killed by strangulation a four-year-old boy and a three-year-old boy.

At age 15 a young woman purposely took steps to lure a nine-year-old girl to her house for the sole purpose of killing her. She had previously tried to kill herself by cutting her wrists and posted on YouTube that her hobbies were killing people and cutting. She also planned other murders. She is still in prison serving a life sentence.

I can't imagine the loneliness of walking around with this disorder as a child. And how unbalancing it would be for a child whose equilibrium is trying to make sense at the same time they have an urge to kill? How much pain are they in?

Revelation 16: The innocent parents

Parents, family and family life are often blamed for the killer's situation. Years ago, mothers of Autistic children were called "refrigerator mothers" and blamed for being cold and unloving. I have found loving parents who are completely confused. One day parents of children or even adults who kill will be vindicated as parents of Autistic children are vindicated today. They are as good or crappy a parent as the rest of us and have done absolutely nothing to cause their loved one to be a killer.

The aunt of a young man who set off bombs to kill people said the family is devastated and broken at the news that our family could be involved in such an awful way. His neighbor said he was quiet, very polite, respectful young man. His grandmother said he was "a loving man from a tight family".

Jeffrey Dahmer's step mother said she cries every night since she learned what happened.

One man I spoke to whose son killed a little girl said his ex-wife was a basket case over what happened.

One father said it was the worst thing that could happen.

CHAPTER 12
Causation, fear and IQ

Sometimes you need to know why. This chapter is for you to understand what I believe to be the cause of prebirth mental disorders.

There is so much to be said for fear. I don't know if the baby in its smallest state can feel the trauma of the Thought that was not placed but if it can feel that happening, it would cause a trauma that is not understood, a fear and an attempt to remove that feeling through escape.

Understanding what causes mental illness was not enough. In my research to understand the "how" of mental illness it always haunted me that I didn't know the "why". That is until I read about a woman doctor who fought to understand why her twin brother had schizophrenia and she did not. They had the same parents. They shared the same womb. And though they were different sexes they were treated equally by their parents.

It was fascinating. What would be the difference that would cause the boy to be so sick and not the girl. As is the story in not only my life but in my research toward understanding mental illness answers fell in my lap. I learned that the umbilical cord could be a problem.

I believe the unborn baby who has a mental illness suffered an instantaneous lack of oxygen and that this oxygen loss occurred at a time when a Thought is being placed. When we suffer a trauma, a severe trauma, we stop all activity for a split second in panic or we run. The trauma from an oxygen loss would cause severe panic in a baby where it has no idea what is happening and where oxygen along with nutrition is everything. This panic can cause a stop in Thought placement. The longer the loss the more Thoughts are not placed leading to multiple mental disorders or syndromes.

If the baby goes into panic mode meaning its Mind may race to find an answer as a person would when in panic mode, this panic can last the lifetime of the person and is usually what is called hyperactivity. This hyperactivity can also cause the person's Mind to "go a mile a minute" leaving the person unable to concentrate, able to concentrate more, or possibly with a high IQ.

The stopping of thought placement and hyperactivity, and hyperactivity in the area of cognition, can happen. This causes simply a missing thought, a missing thought with hyperactivity, a missing thought with a high IQ or any combination of the three.

This is why people with disorders often have a high IQ. Many serial killers have a high IQ. Many people with a high IQ have a disorder like Aspergers.

I know of a child who is a math genius. He graduated college I believe before his teens majoring in mathematics. He is also by his own, his parent's and professional's diagnosis autistic. He once said that he didn't mind his autism because if he wasn't autistic, he wouldn't have the extraordinary math talents that he had.

Fear and injury often cause the person to mentally react and overreact. Fear can make a person run at incredible speeds and have incredible strength. Fear can also cause the fight to be rerouted to the Thoughts dealing with intelligence giving the person an extraordinarily high IQ. This can explain the fact that many with these syndromes and disorders have extraordinarily high IQs with autistic people often being savants.

A word needs to be said for the possibly huge role, of a mental Cytokine Storm.

As I may have already said, it has been said that the reason the Covid-19 virus causes mild cases in some and is fatal for others is due to the Cytokine Storm.

The Cytokine Storm can also happen in the Mind if fear is part of the situation and why wouldn't it be? Loss of oxygen in any being would cause panic. An unborn baby is no different. That baby would be in a state of tremendous fear and disequilibrium and the Mond would fight to return it to its proper state where there is peace.

This fear, just as with the body, would cause an overreaction. This overreaction could have an impact on other parts of the Mind causing not only a higher IQ but an overreaction in other forms like creativity. Sybil had a high IQ along with an extraordinary talent for art. This is not uncommon.

In addition, some patients may be in a constant state of fear and therefore in a constant state of being in the mental equivalent of a cytokine storm as their mental disorder hence ADHD.

An example of a Cytokine Storm in the Mind of an adult would be a person who has Asperger's Syndrome who must speak to a large group of people and does so by bypassing the symptoms of their disorder as best they can. The common reaction in the person would be a mental cytokine storm of fear causing the person to shake or cry

after the speech. Typically, the person would be completely exhausted and have to be away from the cause of the stress, namely people for a while in order to recover.

There needs to be more research and the concepts here need to be developed and refined. The role of stress and fear causing the equivalent of a cytokine storm is one of the situations that should be investigated since a mental cytokine storm could be the cause of many of a patient's symptoms to be exacerbated or to even show up at all as a defense mechanism. It may even be the cause of symptoms of spontaneity.

CHAPTER 13
The **Power** of the Action Thought

Before I tell you about other syndromes or disorders, I need to get the message across to you about the power of the Action Thought. This drive is often called a compulsion and is said to be uncontrollable as you have already heard. The reason it is so strong is because it is part of "The Natural State of Being" that drives the "Task Thought" or the Action Thought in the Task Thought. The drive is natural and therefore powerful.

So much was already written in this book concerning the Action Thought, what it causes and how it feels to the person for whom it is pushing for the Concept Thought to work.

I knew the Action Thought was pushing people to do things and maybe do things that were criminal but, at first, I thought the things that were criminally done because of the Action Thought were against other people and therefore easier to do. People can often do things involving the pain of another easier than doing things causing pain to themselves. But in one disorder the person did things to itself that were just as horrendous like pouring lye in their eyes so that concept of the Action Thought only hurting others became debunked and the Action Thought became understood as something tremendously powerful beyond pain to others or to one's self.

Those with Bennett Syndrome would fall into two categories. Some who had the disorder were defensive and had given up on their morals and heart believing to be born evil. Others were very sad and disappointed in themselves. Wesley Todd wanted to be executed the same way he killed a little boy which was by hanging and in the end of his life he warned others of people like himself and taught how to keep from being killed by people who were like him. Still, he said if he was free, he would do it again.

In my research of all the mental illnesses I could find in order to try to leave no major stone unturned, I came across an illness called BIID which is labeled in the DSM Body Integrity Identity Disorder. This disorder causes the person to injure itself in some of the most severe ways. On top of the severe injury the person is ecstatic to be injured. This tells me that the Action Thought causes so much pain that it is better to actually cut off a leg with a knife or burn one's eyes out than to keep feeling the pain of the Action Thought.

The missing Concept Thought in this illness caused one woman to want to go blind. The Action Thought that could not make the Concept work was so powerful that the Action Thought caused the person to pour lye in her eyes to blind herself. There was a man whose missing Concept Thought made him think he should remove his legs. To do so he placed his legs in a bucket of dry ice to try to force the doctors to have to amputate his legs. This attempt to get rid of what caused the disequilibrium by physically removing what he would consider the source of the problem must have been so horrendously painful. Yet he was not only happy to do it but would have paid great sums of money to have someone in the medical field get the procedure done. You have to ask yourself, how mentally painful could this Action Thought be and how painful is the disequilibrium it causes?

Some call this disorder the Amputee Disorder. Most people who lose their eyesight or their legs are devastated. But the absolute compelling force to become disabled in some way whether its blindness, amputation or whatever causes a tremendous relief. It is not a rush but a release, a freedom and a happiness.

Every "Task Thought" has a Concept Thought and an Action Thought that can wreak havoc with the person if the Concept Thought is missing. Some Thoughts are simply annoying. Some are devastating.

At first, I thought the Action Thought simply turned on the Concept so it could work and the "Task Thought" could complete its task. But I have since learned that the Action Thought has varying degrees of energy and strength. Just like the teenager who gets off the couch to take out the garbage at varying speeds with varying degrees of attention and energy so does the Action Thought do things with more or less speed, attention and energy. It is not a switch.

There are some Action Thoughts that are stronger than others. There are some Action Thoughts that are weaker than others. Right now, we know that the missing Concept Thought causes the Action Thought to activate in its attempt to activate the missing Concept Thought but now we know there is a degree at which it tries and it is different for each person and for each "Task Thought" or for each "Task Thought" according to its importance and use.

In addition, fear and trauma can also make the Action Thought react with more intensity or less intensity. It may also cause the Action Thought to not work at all as well.

The difference in those with no missing Thoughts and with those with missing Thoughts can be due to the Action Thought. The extreme energy in the Action Thought could cause high IQ and by contrast low Action Thought energy could cause low IQ. This is the same with particular talents as well. A person could be extremely good at math, for example, because the Action Thought, possibly due to fear, is very active.

The amount of energy in the Action Thought could account for a person who has a particular missing Thought to have the disorder but do nothing about it or take extreme measures to fill the loss.

VI
So many Syndromes So many illnesses

CHAPTER 14
Syndromes...so far

Oh my God there are more syndromes.

I have labeled all prebirth disorders as syndromes since a syndrome is a number of symptoms occurring together and characterizing a specific disease. Post birth disorders would be simply disorders. Disorders are defined as an irregularity, disturbance or interruption of normal functions.

Sometimes behaviors that seem to be "symptoms" are actually perfectly normal and part of the person's "Natural State of Being" meaning anyone in their situation of having missing Thoughts would act the same way and are correctly reacting to their situation. Being aloof from others if you are unable to understand your own thinking is normal. Being afraid, frustrated, angry, confused when your thoughts make no sense is normal. Being unable to care after a while would be perfectly normal. Being plagued with social anxiety would be normal. Being exhausted after dealing with people would be normal. Being annoyed when someone says they understand and you know they couldn't possibly really understand would be normal. Being sad or depressed over being different from others would be normal. Being someone with few friends would be normal. Many items on the list of symptoms of a particular illness are perfectly normal for a person in that particular circumstance.

Until all mental disorders are understood it may be hard to tell if the disorder was caused by an incident that was before birth or after birth.

The information in this book is based on revelation after revelation and the information is to be used for the purpose of understanding illnesses that are mental as opposed to physical disorders including those disorders that are due to brain injury which disconnects the Thought from the physical body. Mental illnesses are simply nonmaterial illnesses.

One can read this person's case study and that person's case study, this university's study and that university's study and end up with the same conclusion for most mental disorders that they cannot be understood nor can they be cured.

Most of the information in this book was taken not from a list of psychiatric professionals but directly from testimony of the person with the disorder. This provides for purer and more accurate information unadulterated by opinion, personal bias or psychiatric education.

Anything that makes the person less than perfect is an illness no matter how small and seemingly insignificant. This simply means whatever the illness happens to be we need to not act upon it in any negative way and we need to correct it as much as we can.

As you read this you are using things of the Mind and your body is using things of the body. You are not aware of whether your digestive system is currently emptying your stomach or whether your blood vessels are cleaning your blood at a particular place.

You know none of this yet it is all working at full speed, unconsciously and as another world that occupies…YOU.

Mental illnesses are not all from before birth. Some began after birth but all Thoughts that contradict "The Natural State of Being" are illnesses.

Basic human emotions also play a role in mental illness as the person is also human and responsible for its own actions. For the most part those with a mental illness are not responsible for the things directly concerning the mental illness like confusion or the inability to concentrate or pacing for instance or even lack of empathy but would be responsible for what is done as a matter of choice like the choice to either kill or turn one's self in to prevent killing or the choice to take revenge or blame. It is important for the person to understand this since it gives the person the correct perspective in seeing the actual part their choices play and don't play in the mental situation.

Some missing Thoughts are single Thoughts and some are one Thought in a sequential set of Thoughts in "The Natural State of Being" that are to be used one after another as the person grows. Some syndromes have the loss of one Thought allowing the following Thoughts to behave as they should. Some have a loss of every Thought that was to come after the first lost Thought in the series. The loss of one single Thought will cause the person to have different end goals than the loss of all the Thoughts in the entire series.

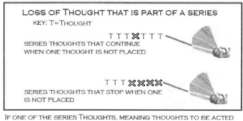

LOSS OF THOUGHT THAT IS PART OF A SERIES
KEY: T=THOUGHT

T T T ✖ T T T
SERIES THOUGHTS THAT CONTINUE
WHEN ONE THOUGHT IS NOT PLACED

T T T ✖ ✖ ✖ ✖
SERIES THOUGHTS THAT STOP WHEN ONE
IS NOT PLACED

IF ONE OF THE SERIES THOUGHTS, MEANING THOUGHTS TO BE ACTED UPON ONE ANOTHER, IS MISSING IT CAN STOP ONLY THAT THOUGHT OR ALL THOUGHTS AFTER THAT THOUGHT.

The disorders listed, though they may have other names in the Psychiatric field, have their own names here because the way of approaching, understanding and healing each disorder is different than in the Psychiatric world. Giving the syndromes and disorders their own names gives them credence and allows one to see the disorder from a new and different point of view.

What caused each syndrome in the baby will be stated here as much as possible so that the situation could be understood.

Those syndromes that have added spectrums or added types as labeled in the DSM, I believe to be the same disorder that is felt by people who are different. Some are hyperactive. Some are more subdued. Some are vengeful. Some are, though it may be hard to believe, as kind as they can be and so on.

Corpal Syndrome

Prebirth Missing Thought: UNKNOWN (single Thought possibly visibility of self)

Prebirth injury: Loss of Concept Thought, intact Action Thought

Reaction to injury: Drive to replace the missing Thought with another person's fear.

Thought group: Love

Possible connected street name: None but causes child abuse and rape, possible bondage (as a mental disorder)

"You know, you'll hear psychologists will say that rape is a crime about power and control. That's not accurate. Power and control are a means to an end. What turned me on is fear." - Colorado serial rapist

This syndrome causes the person to desire or need to see fear in another and often, if not always, to have to be the one to cause that fear. The use of threats of murder and/or rape and the use of tools of torture are often a part of the person's drive. It is typical that murder and rape follow or are part of the act of causing fear.

The main goal is not to kill or even to rape though the act of causing fear may cause sexual arousal and sexual arousal in a normal relationship may not be able to be achieved due to lack of fear. The main goal and maybe the only goal would be to cause fear. The acts of rape, murder, child abuse by caretaker, torture and bondage can be part of this disorder.

Corpal Syndrome is a mental disorder that begins in the unborn baby in the Prebirth stage of development between conception and the time when the baby is able to sustain itself as a viable life form. Corpal Syndrome is a disorder that causes the person to attempt to replace the Concept Thought by causing fear in another since only fear that is in another will bring that relief.

Damage to the unborn baby blocks a Thought that was to be placed in the Mind causing loss and mental pain. The type of Thought that is missing is currently unknown but it may have to do with the Concept of being "visible" since fear would give the person complete attention.

What the missing Thought truly is needs to be revealed before the right Thought can be assigned. This disorder has caused the person to engage in abuse, rapes and murders that are random and linked to fear.

Corpal Syndrome is one of the disorders caused by the missing Concept Thought part of the "Task Thought". This, as in Bennett Syndrome, leaves the Action Thought part of the "Task Thought" to fight for its survival and create the overwhelming drive to fulfill the task. It is that drive that causes the need to cause and maybe see fear in another person and that fear has to be genuine to feel relief. In other words, a crime or painful situation probably has to take place.

Because Corpal Syndrome is a disorder that begins before birth it is as deep and infiltrating as it could possibly be Corpal Syndrome causes:

- A mental drive
- Lack of control over the Thought: "I am a violent predator and I am out of control. I've been out of control for a long time… After a while the f---ing monster kicks in." Psychiatrist about rapist: "He never won any of these battles with the monster."
- Feels it as a child: "had rape fantasies even as a child". A victim said of the rapist, "He said he had that urge for as long as he could remember and he tried to fight for as long as he could then one day, he just gave in."
- A belief that causing fear in another will relieve the pain probably of disequilibrium.
- Behavior with no understanding of the cause:
- Unlike Bennett Syndrome may feel badly for his victims. "He covered me with a blanket because I was shivering."
- An abnormal sexual situation because the person needs the partner to be fearful.
- Relief at causing fear stated by convicted rapist: "I got some satisfaction…it was like I'd just eaten Thanksgiving dinner". (I would like to note that the satisfaction here is not the satisfaction of getting something but removing something. A good example would be a soldier who was a smoker who was without cigarettes on the battlefield for months gets a cigarette and feels good about smoking that cigarette because it relieves the still nagging physical and psychological need).
- As with Bennett Syndrome the person will sometimes keep what forensic psychologists call trophies. The items are to remind of the situation to cause relief. The keeping of reminders is not always the case since a journal or reminder would not be needed if the victim was readily available as in the case of parental abuse or kidnapped victims.

Studies have been done for decades on those who behave according to the symptoms of Corpal Syndrome revealing little if anything. This is due to the fact that Corpal Syndrome is not a physical disorder nor is it a post birth disorder but rather a prebirth disorder.

Corpal Syndrome does not affect learning in any way. Those with Corpal Syndrome can have anywhere from low IQ levels to extremely high IQ levels and can, at times, be found in higher economic or status positions. Those with Corpal Syndrome know right from wrong and are intellectually able to follow rules and the law.

Corpal Syndrome is a disorder where the sufferer lives a basically normal and often productive life between outbreaks except for possible lack of arousal during sex. When the outbreaks occur, they hit hard and the sufferer behaves in an extremely bizarre and often dangerous manner. This, normal until horrendously bizarre, situation causes those around the sufferer to say they had no clue the person would do the things they did and often to be in denial of such behavior. Those with Corpal Syndrome feel a loss that is debilitating when it hits and take action in order to relieve the pain in ways they cannot explain. Some call the feelings they have a fantasy but it is not.

As with many Syndromes from the Prebirth stage there are sometimes other Prebirth disabilities that accompany Corpal Syndrome causing the sufferer to do even more unrelated and bizarre things. Often, those who suffer with Corpal Syndrome will have additional issues in the field of Psychology and will often use what Freud called defense mechanisms. Prejudice can be present as well as revenge and blame. Confusion and repeatedly expressing differing reasons for their behavior is common since the person has no clue why they are so driven and is trying to find out as well.

Often the person can commit crimes to relieve the situation with prostitutes using the excuse that they are below human. Sometimes they will consider themselves to be Satan.

I know of three situations where I believe the mother to have had Corpal Syndrome. One was the story of Sybil. One was in the story where a boy was chained to a toilet all day and made to sleep chained up. The third is of a man who was hit in the stomach with a hammer, was threatened with his finger being put in a light socket and stabbed in the tongue with a knife. None of these were killed.

Indications of Corpal Syndrome

- Desire for basic random fear-based abuse, killing or rape.
- The logical unconscious conclusion that to cause fear in another will relieve the loss.
- Extreme feeling of a loss at a very early age with no opposing memory for comparison.
- Awareness of the loss and a feeling of being very different from other human beings.
- Awareness that others do not have the loss.
- Psychological behaviors from the feeling of loss such as anger, revenge, jealousy, blame.
- Extreme desire to fill the loss to the point of endangering themselves and/or others.
- The actions of alcoholism, drug use, suicide, serial killing, serial rape, murder.
- Possible domestic violence.
- Desire or need to abuse a child.

-
-
-
-
-
-
-
-
-
-
-
-
-
-
-

Farrell Syndrome

Prebirth Missing Thought: General Love for others (single Thought)

Prebirth injury: Loss of Concept Thought and Action Thought.

Reaction to injury: lack of love, connection and empathy toward anyone who is not connected to the person's self or in the person's self-circle.

Thought group: Love

Possible connected street name: Psychopathy/Sociopathy

"She'll cut your head off and not even know you're bleeding."

This syndrome presents in various ways depending on the person's choices and ambitions. The range of behaviors can go from murder where the person will kill for a quarter or a bit of recognition to someone who looks and behaves normally most of the time but takes steps others would not because of their lack of care about the impact such behavior would have on others. The range of this disorder was a shocking revelation as I had always been led to believe that this disorder referred only to those who would commit horrendous crimes. I now know that this disorder is very widespread and involves a huge percentage of the population.

Farrell Syndrome is a mental disorder that begins in the unborn baby in the Prebirth stage of development between conception and the time when the baby is able to sustain itself as a viable life form making it a Prebirth disorder. Farrell Syndrome is a disorder that usually causes no mental pain or depression but not always.

Damage to the unborn baby blocks a Thought that was supposed to be placed in the Mind that is the Thought of empathy. The Thought of empathy follows the Thought of egocentricity that the child is born with causing the person to stay in the stage of egocentricity. The loss is of the complete "Task Thought", meaning the Concept Thought and Action Thought of the "Task Thought" are both missing, making the "Task Thought" nonexistent. In other words they never have feelings for someone who is not in their circle of self.

Many Prebirth disorders where the Concept Thought is missing, but the Action Thought is intact, cause pain and an enormous drive. This disorder does not have pain or a drive attached since the Action Thought is also missing but that doesn't mean the person doesn't know something is very wrong and try to seek help or relief.

If the Action Thought is active the person may experience a sadness, an irritation or a depression along with a desire to be like others or they may just accept the situation. "I don't emote", said a professional journalist nonchalantly. The Concept Thought of Love of self may simply be fulfilling enough.

The problem comes in when the person is angry, mean, vengeful and so on. A problem also comes in when the person wants something that is blocked by another person. This disorder is an open door to other emotions that can cause horrendous situations. Many politicians have this disorder allowing them to take actions that are contrary to their constituents. Mob bosses often have this disorder.

Farrell Syndrome causes the person to be able to do anything no matter how immoral to get something they want, even if they only slightly want it, like killing someone who simply annoys them or they feel is not worthy of being on the planet. They may do things that are illegal with an awareness that there could be legal consequences but if they have connections and do not believe they will have any legal consequences, they will probably do what they please. This person could go as far as to kill someone who gets in their way or who simply annoys them. They may look down at others and those they look down at most are more dispensable such as prostitutes and people who are weak. It is often stated that the person with this disorder has love for family or friends and therefore cannot have a complete loss of empathy for people or could not have committed a crime.

What is not understood is that in "The Natural State of Being", in this category of Thoughts the unborn baby is given two separate "Task Thoughts". One planted Thought is of love of self and the other planted Thought is of love of others. Love of self includes not only the self, but those who would be considered by the person to be part of that self. These are two separate Thoughts. Pets would be considered part of the self as well.

If a person or even an animal betrays the person, it is no longer in the "self" circle or part of the "self". This allows the person with Farrell Syndrome to attack any person who was formerly part of the "self" if the person wishes to do so.

An instance of this is the person who takes good care of their children until the children get in the way of a desire, something the self wants. The children then move out of the "self" circle allowing the person to get rid of the children to fulfill a desire. People who killed their children because they want to keep a new boyfriend or girlfriend who did not want kids would be an example. Chris Watts and Susan Smith types would be examples.

One example I found was of a man who lost his job and stole money from his mother to support his family. After not being able to find a job the people in the "self" category including his mother became a threat to that self and therefore the enemy and they were unknowingly removed from the circle. This allowed him to be able to kill his entire family, run away and start a new family. That family would live unless it got in the way and fell out of the self's circle.

After being caught and ending up in prison one man stated that he was sorry he killed his family. I believe he was sorry only because he was caught and being punished. He was sorry for the person in the "self" namely him, and possibly for the hurt he caused his new family if they were still in the "self" circle.

Love of self

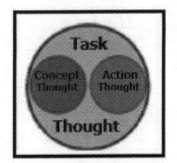

Task Thought of Love of Self
completely intact

Love of others

Task Thought of Love of others missing
Concept Thought and Action Thought

Those who are considered part of the Love of Self can be removed by betraying the person. This removal is done on an unconscious level and can lead to disastrous things.

The person's individuality plays a part in Farrell Syndrome. There are people who are right brained dominant, meaning they are more social and creative. There are people who are more left brained dominant, who are more detail oriented. An example of a right brained person is an actor, musician or a politician. An example of a left brained person is a politician, lawyer, a scientist, or an accountant. Of course, there are people who are in the middle as well.

A person who is right brained with Farrell Syndrome would be friendly, funny, artistic, and able to tell a joke as they picked your pocket. This person could be considered a sociopath.

A person who is left brained with Farrell Syndrome would be legalistic, boring, and unable to tell a joke. This person could be considered a psychopath.

Those with this disorder, like many with mental illnesses, can also be highly intelligent making the ability for those around the person to be unaware of the loss of empathy, until it is undeniably obvious.

Farrell Syndrome Symptoms:

- Lack of cognizance of feelings or needs of others or their rights.
- Considered to have no conscience.
- No respect for social norms or laws since these usually connect to fairness with others.
- Lies, deceives others for personal gain.
- Behaves without thinking of consequences often because they can easily talk themselves out of most consequences having no conscience and no fear of getting caught.
- Shows aggressive or aggravated behavior especially if someone challenges their concept of what should be.
- Irresponsible.
- Shows no feeling of guilt or remorse for having harmed or mistreated others because others don't matter.
- Could be considered "cold" showing no emotions or investment in the lives of others.
- May use humor, intelligence, or charisma to manipulate others.

- Since the "self" Thought is intact and unchallenged the person will have a sense of superiority and strong, unwavering opinions.
- Will attempt to control others by intimidating or threatening them.
- Since the feeling of fairness to others is missing, will get into frequent legal trouble or perform criminal acts.
- Will take risks at the expense of themselves or others thinking they will talk their way out of it.
- Will threaten suicide without ever acting on those threats.
- Will stay in the stage of Egocentrism.
- May become addicted to drugs, alcohol, or other substances.

It needs to be noted that contrast often causes learning. Those with this disorder do not have a contrasting Thought. Therefore, since this starts early the child may stay in the stage of egocentricity for its entire life causing the person to be able to do extremely selfish things with no remorse.

Ibach Syndrome

Prebirth Missing Thought: Concept of self as a child (single Thought)

Prebirth injury: Loss of Concept Thought with Action Thought overactive or intact.

Reaction to injury: lack of concept of the child in the person's self

Thought group: Truth

Possible connected street name: Pedophilia (as a mental disorder)

"There is an emptiness, a void in them".

Ibach Syndrome is a mental disorder that begins in the unborn baby in the Prebirth stage of development between conception and the time when the baby is able to sustain itself as a viable life form making Ibach Syndrome a Prebirth disorder. Ibach Syndrome is a disorder that often causes depression, and/or guilt in the sufferer.

Damage to the unborn baby blocks a Thought of the concept a child should have of itself as a child that was to be placed in the Mind causing a mental disorder. The loss is of the Concept Thought in the "Task Thought" unit while the Action continues to push for completion.

Many prebirth disorders where the Concept Thought is missing, but the Action Thought is intact, may cause an enormous drive. This disorder causes the sufferer to feel an extreme need to do things that he/she would not normally do and basically does not want to do. This disorder can present itself as an attraction to children with the temptation to have sexual relations with children. It sometimes leads to murder to protect the person or to try to fulfill what wasn't fulfilled with sex.

People with Ibach Syndrome fall into two categories. One is that they do not want to act on the drive caused by the Action Thought and have chosen not to do so. There are organizations where the person has Pedophilia (Ibach syndrome), but with the help of others with the same Thought impulses does not act on them. The other category is one where they have given up or never thought to fight it and simply act on the Thought that comes from thinking to replace the missing Thought with a child.

Those with Ibach Syndrome are fully aware that any action they take to fulfill the "urge" which we know as a missing Thought by molesting a child would be illegal. They are also aware that it will hurt another person probably for life and that it will cause pain to other families and their own families. And, it would probably ruin their life as well.

"When I hear other pedophiles tell me that they are even relatively happy in life, I sometimes am tempted to ask them what f..king planet they live on. How in the world can anyone go through everyday living with this curse and not want to fling themselves off the nearest bridge on a daily basis"? -40-year-old pedophile

"I look back on it now and find it amazing that I never got to the point where I picked up a gun and ended it. There were days when I got up and it was all I could think about. I'd tell myself I just want to die. I just want to die all day for days on end." -42-year-old pedophile

What is not understood is that in "The Natural State of Being", in the category of Truth, there is a concept of what a child is that enters the being from the beginning to be activated at the time the being becomes a child. The progression is baby (not conscious) to toddler (not conscious) to child (conscious) to teenager (conscious) to adult (conscious). If the Concept of being a child was not placed in the unborn baby as part of the program to be activated later, the child will not see itself as what the concept of a child is. At that time the Action Thought will kick in and the child will desire that the Concept of what a child is will be acted upon. Since that Concept is missing the child will, as with Bennett Syndrome, Astore Syndrome and others, replace the missing Concept with another.

With this disorder, replacement is unconsciously believed to be achieved by bringing a real child as close as possible to the person to replace the child concept that is missing. Since sex is an intimate act, this would be done by having sex with a child. The replacement is often with sex as sex is an intimate action and in extreme cases sometimes it is believed as well that killing the replacement child brings the person closer to the child and will fulfill the missing Thought.

Sometimes eating the replacement is the course of action, but this is rare as usually sex with the child works for temporary relief. The goal is to get the replacement to be as much a part of the self as possible to replace the missing Concept Thought.

This replacement behavior can happen at a very young age because Ibach Syndrome is a Prebirth disorder. The person would feel they are missing the child when it is time for them to be the child. This is why some child molesting is done by other children.

Many who say they are pedophiles would say they watched porn and that was the cause of their problems. As with the keeping of "trophies" in Bennett Syndrome, watching porn is a medication. In Bennett Syndrome, the person would kill another and keep a reminder of its effect on them when acting to replace the missing Concept Thought due to Bennett Syndrome. With Ibach Syndrome the person keeps trophies of a child or pictures of having sex with a child.

Watching porn for pedophiles is a way of temporarily and superficially replacing the missing child Concept by bringing a child close to the person through the closest thing, which is sex even if it is just an image. The problem is, as with Bennett Syndrome and many syndromes, it either does not work to remove the need or works only temporarily. This attempt to fix the problem by watching porn makes matters worse and reminds the person they need something and are not getting it. It is a temporary fix like drinking alcohol. When the alcohol is gone or when the porn is gone, the problem still remains.

At the point that the person realizes they are a pedophile and possible child molester, they may try to do something to stop it like suicide. Many go to psychiatrists prior to suicide, but no psychiatrist can help them without understanding the origin of the problem, which is that the disorder is a missing Thought from before birth.

Most pedophiles look like and act like others in the community and this disorder cannot be detected through normal everyday actions.

In addition, since there is typically no cognitive disorder connected to this syndrome, those who act to ease the drive from this syndrome and commit child molestation are responsible for their actions and will often do whatever they can to escape prosecution including using any defensive mechanisms available to them and possibly committing murder. Personality traits and defense tactics are not part of this syndrome and those with this syndrome have the capacity to obey the law and not hurt a child.

Because this occurs at the time when the concept of the child should come into awareness this syndrome can take priority over whatever will come next in the series as part of "The Natural State of Being". In other words, relieving the missing Concept Thought of a child is what is most important before the Concept Thought of being a teenager or adult can happen but the Concept Thought of being a teenager or adult may still happen.

Not moving on with the next Thoughts in the series may cause the person to be sexually stunted for their entire lives. However, in the case of Ibach Syndrome, sometimes the rest of the series continues, and the person can live a normal life with a sexual attraction to an adult and love for their own family in a nonsexual way along with the urge to be with children.

It needs to be noted that some who are attracted to children for a relationship or for a relationship that includes sex may consider themselves unable to have a relationship with those of the same intellect or maturity meaning another adult so they are attracted to children. These people are not suffering from Ibach Syndrome or pedophilia. This sometimes occurs when a person is slightly cognitively slow but is either not aware that they are slow or do not want to face that they belong in that category or are a part of those people.

Astore Syndrome

Prebirth Missing Thought: The concept of the child as its own sex (single Thought, series Thought)

Prebirth injury: Loss of Concept Thought with Action Thought in tact

Symptoms: Drive to have a sexual or intimate relationship with those of the same se

Thought group: Life

Possible connected street name: Homosexuality/bisexuality (as a mental disorder)

Note: The definition of sex here is not in reference intercourse but to reference to the behavioral characteristics and functional structure that distinguishes males from females.

Astore Syndrome will cause the person to pursue a sexual/intimate relationship with a person or persons of the same sex.

The importance of this particular Thought cannot be understated. Most of the other Task Thoughts placed in the child are for the growth of the individual child. This Task Thought, however, is for the existence of all mankind. It is at the core of the existence of the human race. Love for the being's self in general including love for its self as its sex is vital for not only the race but for the race as human as made in "The Natural State of Being".

Love of one's self in all things is part of the unit that is the core of mankind. It makes us not just animals who mate but humans who are of a more noble purpose.

Astore Syndrome is a mental disorder that begins in the unborn baby in the Prebirth stage of development between conception and the time when the baby is able to sustain itself as a viable life form. Astore Syndrome is a missing Thought disorder that has to do with one of the central most important parts of the core of the self which is the person loving its self as its own sex.

As a child who is loved beyond human comprehension, the child would be made to love all of its self. That would be its "Natural State of Being". Loving its self would include loving its self as its sex. Those who are not missing this Thought have a hard time understanding the substitution since it is at the core of one's being. Though they may not like certain things about their body what they don't like is not central to their core. Those who do not have this disorder cannot understand the substitution of this core Thought.

Though the Concept Thought is gone, the Action Thought part of this particular "Task Thought", whose job or task is to act out all the things it takes to be a male or female in the being of that person, is still active. Therefore, if there is a missing Concept Thought, the Action Thought causes an unconscious need to replace the missing Concept Thought just as it did in Bennett Syndrome. The Action Thought is fighting to fulfill its task of being the person loved and seen as someone of that sex.

This replacement of the Concept Thought is done by replacing it with another person as it was with Bennett Syndrome where the person would replace the missing Concept Thought with the life of another but here it replaces it with the sex of another.

As you know, at the stage before memory is formed Thoughts are systematically placed in the Mind of the unborn child in a specific pattern to be used after birth. These "Task Thoughts" allow the child to perform a particular task and each "Task Thought" performs its task over and over throughout the child's life. In the case of Astore Syndrome the task is to be a female or a male according to the plan in "The Natural State of Being".

When one specific Thought is not placed intact in the unborn child's Mind due to currently unknown or unconfirmed circumstances a disorder will occur. Astore Syndrome is one of the disorders caused by the missing Concept part of the "Task Thought" as in Bennett Syndrome. This leaves the Action part of the "Task Thought" to fight for the survival and fulfillment of the task and creates the overwhelming drive to do its job.

Since it is "The Natural State of Being" and part of the mental plan for a child to form an attachment and love for its self as its own sex, then the child doing so would be normal and healthy. In other words, the child's love for one of its own sex is natural. The person is supposed to wholeheartedly love someone of their own sex. Replacing the being for another of the same sex or gender would be the disorder.

In the case of Astore Syndrome the missing Concept Thought in this disorder would cause unusual attachments to a person of the same sex including possible sexual attachments.

Because Astore Syndrome is a disorder that begins before birth it is as deep and infiltrating as it could possibly be.

Astore Syndrome causes:

- A feeling of something wrong or amiss.
- Lack of control.
- Behavior with no understanding of the cause.
- Possible feeling of emptiness or loss.
- Attachment to one of the same sex.

One characteristic of Astore Syndrome, as in all Prebirth disorders, is that the person behaves in a way that they cannot explain. This behavior can alter the person's life and lead them in directions they don't want to go. When asked why they behave as they do, the person with Astore Syndrome will truthfully answer that they have no idea. This is because there was no memory from before the disorder happened as purposely retrievable memory had not yet been formed.

Studies have been done for decades on those who behave according to the symptoms of Astore Syndrome including brain scans revealing nothing unusual. Astore Syndrome, being a mental disorder, is only visible by observation of the behavior of the person or their testimonies. Behaviors sometimes show early in life but most often later in life or in the adult. As with all disorders where there is a missing Concept Thought, the person's "Natural State of Being" will fight to replace the Thought.

The child is made a particular sex. Along with that physical sex, the child is given many non-physical Concepts that are linked to that sex. Part of the sex Thought progression is as follows. The Concept to love itself as a person in general is placed in the unborn baby as its "Natural State of Being" and shows in its egocentric state. The Concept to love its sex is placed, probably around the same time that love of its self is placed, as its "Natural State of Being" to be activated at the proper time later in the child's life. Also planted is the Concept to love one who is the opposite sex as its "Natural State of Being" to be activated many years later at the proper time with loving one of the opposite sex or gender being the ultimate goal for survival of the human race.

Just as in learning, any progression follows a pattern. The baby uses a rattle and is fascinated with it until that rattle has provided all the learning the baby needs and the baby moves on to more intelligent things. The baby crawls until something better comes along like walking. Walking is the ultimate end goal.

The baby is, for a long time, unaware of its sex and just performs tasks simply as a being. There is no thought or concept or understanding of anything concerning sex in a baby. They are egocentric meaning the love for themselves as a being is being expressed and growing as it should. Many times, when a young child falls and doesn't get hurt, it will cry because it is insulted and not because of any injury. This is the Concept of the being loving itself as part of its "Natural State of Being".

This disorder has been misdiagnosed for many years as a disorder in the attraction of a person of one sex toward a person of the same sex. The love and attraction of a person to a person of the same sex is, in fact, part of "The Natural State of Being". This disorder is a disorder not of

113

loving one of one's own sex but to whom the love is linked. It is not whether there is an attraction but to whom. The attraction to one's own sex is "The Natural State of Being". The problem occurs when the person's attraction to one of their own sex is not them. This misunderstanding has caused this disorder to continue to be hidden over centuries. Those with Astore Syndrome often feel a loss that is constant but unconscious and take action in order to relieve the feeling in ways they cannot explain.

Astore Syndrome has an additional problem of loss of equilibrium and possibly self-esteem which may play a part in the behaviors of the person.

Indications of Astore Syndrome

- Feeling of being different at a very early age with no opposing memory for comparison.
- Confusion due to loss of equilibrium
- A feeling as if something is continually blocking what they are or want to be.
- An extreme feeling of being pulled emotionally and sexually.
- Possible low self-esteem especially since they may feel they are not up to what they believe they should be.
- The drive to be unusually close to one of the same sex or gender including sexual encounters.
- Possible psychological behaviors from the feeling of loss such as anger, revenge, jealousy, blame.
- Possible need to fill the loss to the point of hurting themselves and/or others.
- Depression.
- An unusual attraction to color.
- The actions of alcoholism, drug use and suicide.
- Sometimes a childlike voice mixed with an adult voice

It needs to be noted that Astore Syndrome is a disorder from the loss of a Concept Thought that is part of a cluster of Thoughts in a series. The injury can cause the Concept Thought to be gone and take with it all or some of the rest of the Thoughts in the series or it can cause only the Concept Thought to be gone while keeping the other Thoughts of the series intact. If more of the Thoughts in the series after the Concept Thought that is missing are gone as well, it will cause more behaviors than just an attraction to another person of the same sex.

If the unconscious Concept Thought of sex is not placed and there is no other loss of Thoughts connected to that loss the person may simply be attracted to one of its own sex and that will be the only difference in the person. All connecting traits will stay intact.

However, since the sex series consists of not only the concept of sex meaning male or female but all that would go with being male or female other behaviors may arise.

In "The Natural State of Being" series a male would also have the concept of boy (male child) and the concept of man (male adult) and a female would have the concept of girl (female child) and the concept of woman (female adult). If the series stopped the child would not relate to them and their traits.

In males being male connects predominately to the concept of less pliable less soft, less emotional strength, mental strength and fatherliness where in girls being female connects predominately to the concept of kindness, loving strength and motherliness. These traits, of course, are not mutually exclusive but are more dominant for each sex.

If the Concept Thought of sex is gone in the child it may believe that it has no traits of its sex whatsoever or few traits of its sex. It may believe it will never be a man or woman in the strongest sense. It also may stay a child because it does not consider itself to possibly be a man or woman. It is understandable since the Concept was lost so early.

Children like things of color as any advertiser of children's toys can tell you. Therefore, if the loss of the Concept Thought kept the person thinking at a young age a person could have an unexplainable connection to things that are colorful, think Liberace or Elton John for example or other colorful entertainers. Some of the child's sex traits go on and some stay in the same place.

A male may walk or talk like a prissy woman and a female may walk or talk like a tough man because they lost the concept of their sex and the perceived or real traits that go with that sex. This leaves their true sex so from them that they don't feel like they have those traits or don't feel like their own sex.

In addition, the Concept of attraction to the opposite sex could be intact but the need for fulfillment of their own sex Concept Thought would come first as it was supposed to be activated before any attraction to the opposite sex.

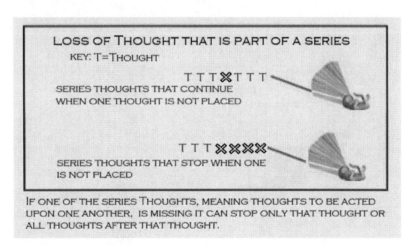

LOSS OF THOUGHT THAT IS PART OF A SERIES

KEY: T=THOUGHT

T T T ✖ T T T

SERIES THOUGHTS THAT CONTINUE
WHEN ONE THOUGHT IS NOT PLACED

T T T ✖✖✖✖

SERIES THOUGHTS THAT STOP WHEN ONE
IS NOT PLACED

IF ONE OF THE SERIES THOUGHTS, MEANING THOUGHTS TO BE ACTED UPON ONE ANOTHER, IS MISSING IT CAN STOP ONLY THAT THOUGHT OR ALL THOUGHTS AFTER THAT THOUGHT.

Edson Syndrome

Prebirth Missing Thought: loss of the foundational Thought of the individual self as part of a whole of humanity that lives under the same laws that cause behavior as other humans. In other words, loss of the Thought that we are all foundationally the same.

Prebirth injury: floundering to live among people they feel they don't understand because they believe they are different. Lack of relating one's feelings to the fact that others would feel the same. Automatically seeing others as being different therefore having to pretend they are the same. Lack of placement of Thought of the connection of the self to others that contains the set of compassion based logical rules for human interaction.

Symptoms: feeling of separation from others, misunderstanding the thoughts and actions of others, reliance on other things that do not use the lost Thoughts for daily living, fear of having to perform without understanding the laws of humanity.

Thought group: Love

Possible connected street name: Autism/Asperger's Syndrome

Reaction to Injury: Belief they have to fake their humanity to fit in, belief that they are different when they are not, copy how others behave,

"Mom, am I an alien?"

Edson Syndrome is a before birth disorder that causes a lack of understanding of the mentally based physical set of Thoughts that nonverbally express what the person is thinking. The injury happens in the baby between conception and birth before purposeful conscious memory is formed. This set is part of a schema meaning the Thoughts work together.

Single Thoughts or multiple Thoughts in the set can be missing as can the whole set.

Edson Syndrome is a disorder that causes the person to be forced to live with people they feel they do not understand. This is because, due to injury, they did not have part or all of the Concept Thought of their nonmaterial or mental "self" and the actions and emotions that go with it which can be seen in others. Within this setoff Thoughts of the mental self would lie all the gestures and unspoken laws of being a social person.

There are different situations connected to this syndrome. This set of Thoughts contains many Thoughts that are completely intact in the person with no disorder. Loss of one Thought or loss to multiple Thoughts due to injury makes this loss considered to be part of a spectrum. In reality it is just a bunch of thoughts that may or may not be working.

Because this is due to an injury and the injury can cause fear which can account for other traits like sensitivity to light and sound.

Sometimes this loss is accompanied by loss of other cognitive Thoughts due to injury. Though the original loss in the Thought set is the same for all in this situation which Thoughts are affected may vary. In addition, any other losses that are attached can make it seem like this disorder has many aspects. For example, the loss of this main Thought accompanied by another loss in the Sensorimotor stage would be different than a loss in the sensorimotor stage alone and different from a loss of this main Thought alone. The loss of this main Thought or any part of it along with any other loss seems to make a different illness but, in reality, it doesn't.

The loss of this Thought can be accompanied by the loss of any Thought at any stage. Because of this the person can have this disorder and have many differing Thought losses at various cognitive stages. A person with this disorder can be one who just sits and rocks or twirls a string or one who seems to be fine and anywhere in between.

In addition, when the loss of a Thought happens, it could and often does cause a hyperactivity of other Thoughts. The energy from the lost Thought or from the fear could transfer to another Thought. A good example is seriation, the developmental Thought that deals with organizing. This is where the child will gain great pleasure from the organization of things and from actions like putting objects in a row in the early child and organizing books that are in Roman numerals within Roman numerals typically in the adult. This sense of organization is actually a part of "The Natural State of Being" so it becomes very important to the child and any change in the lines it is forming with its blocks or the drawing it makes will cause a major emotional upset. This Thought of seriation explains the calendar savants who can tell you the day of a particular date a hundred years in the past or future. It is from this Thought of seriation that you would get a "Rainman' who is great with numbers.

So, this disorder can have not only the loss of the concept of the nonmaterial self and the lack of understanding the concept of other nonmaterial persons that goes along with it but can have any host of additional losses added to the situation. Cognitive issues can play a role making the child unable to do so many things like speak, for example. On the other hand, it has its gifts. One man said he wouldn't have become a Rubik's Cube champion if he didn't have autism.

Facial expressions are a planned Thought in "The Natural State of Being" that is part of the nonmaterial self Thought, but if that Thought is not planted, a person would not know what to do and when to do it unless they were taught each expression. It would be like meeting an animal in the woods that one has never seen. Is it friendly? What do its actions mean? Do I run? Do I stand still? How would you know? You wouldn't.

Social norms like how far we should stand from each other, how we should look at each other, how we know if the other person is happy, how we know if the other person is sad, etc. may not be there.

The lack of being able to socially interact is the strongest issue with this disorder but there are other symptoms of Edson Syndrome as well. Those symptoms are really reactions to the main part of the disorder and accompanying lost Thoughts. These symptoms are: to have little eye contact, to prefer to be alone, to have an attachment to objects or animals, to act oddly like yell or shake their hands called stimming, to make odd noises, to pace, to have extraordinary talents as a savant, to have few friends, to be unable to talk, to have communication problems in every area, to become frustrated, and in higher functioning people to be depressed, to try to pretend to fit in to the world of people who don't have this disorder called masking, to become exhausted when trying to mask, to avoid any social setting, to zone out when masking gets too exhausting.

A great explanation of what it would be like to have this disorder is to imagine you have to play a video game and it would be best for your life if you won. This video game has rules but you don't know them. You know how to manipulate the character in your game. You know to move your little lever to the right so your character goes right and to the left so your character goes left. You know to press one button to jump and another to use your sword.

You can manipulate your character any way you want, but you don't know why. You don't know who the good guys are and who the bad guys are. You don't know why you are walking in the first place. You don't know what it is you are trying to achieve. You don't know any rules except how to move your character. That is somewhat this disorder.

The Scenario:

The baby is floating in warmth and love and maybe it hears a few nice sounds.

The Thought of Assimilation and Accommodation has been planted with Assimilation activating first and Accommodation to activate second.

The Thought of the nonmaterial self as an entity with the Thoughts needed to interact with others is placed and activated unless there is an injury and the Thought Concept of the nonmaterial self and its components had not been placed.

Sudden unexplained squeezing gives the entity the Thought of not only being a physical entity but an entity with a body that is connected to its Mind and it is now a unit unless the Thought of the mental self in the entity is not placed. So, the "me" has a body that is connected to a still primitive Mind.

The baby may unconsciously try to make what sense it can out of the unusual squeezing and of course gets nowhere because it doesn't have the Thought of the environment yet. It can use its Mind as it relates to objects but does not have a concept other than that relationship. This object concept that it can understand also includes pets.

Without the Thought of the nonmaterial or mental self for the entity there is just squeezing of the body so confusion and fear may very easily set in.

Upon birth, sudden explosive lights, sounds, smells and touching are experienced. If there is already fear, these things are added to the fear and confusion that has entered its world with no recourse, understanding or prior memory and without the major component of the Thought of the nonmaterial mental self. Just like the fear of a shotgun blast for a veteran causes spontaneous fear so does the things thrust on the baby in its new nonwatery no longer dark warm world.

119

Due to the injury the fear in the child's life may be exacerbated because of all the stimulus and there is no concept of time so what is happening has no end. Therefore, a mental Cytokine storm of fear and desire for escape can happen.

The whole concept of being a mental "me" is lost as is what would have been the new mental "me's" connection to other mental "me persons". It doesn't know anything about its own "me" so it doesn't know of your "you".

Input of the child's senses are remembered as an extreme fear of input from the senses. This can often cause the child to remember things of the senses as a sensitivity to say the least. This so-called sensitivity to light and sound is often spoken of by family and the person themselves. Sometimes this sensitivity is extreme causing the child great distress.

The world the baby had been thrown into is one of fear if it has no Concept of its nonmaterial self. But the senses are not the only input upon birth. The input of faces and eyes is one if the baby is fearful can be just as scary since the mental self is not there to relate. This is why faces and eyes are later avoided. Facial gestures would be linked to the face and eyes that would have already been rejected.

This situation, as you should fully understand by now, is all encompassing and all the baby knows. It is living in a world of possible fear and confusion with no sense of time and with input that should have been connected to the nonmaterial self and the self of others but couldn't be. If disequilibrium is activated at this time, it would be felt throughout the entire life of the child. I hope it is not.

The loss of a Thought causes other things to happen in the world of Thought. It causes a Thought to not be placed. It causes fear, confusion and possible disequilibrium. It may cause a distress if the lack of oxygen is the cause of the lost Thought as I believe. It may cause mental hyperactivity in other Thoughts.

Fear happens when some Thoughts are stopped but often it causes more energy to be sent to other Thoughts like math cognition for example. This causes the phenomenon called being a savant.

This energy burst makes interest in particular objects like trains, Rubrics Cube or math allowing the situation of savantism to emerge. Just as a fear of a gun blast for war veterans causes a spontaneous burst of energy so does the fear caused by the loss of a Thought.

The "Task Thought" to succeed is a Thought planted and activated early on in all of us. It would be mixed with the Thought to escape in this situation causing running, hand flapping which is all the baby knows and various types of actions. An example of the drive for success is in the act of lighting a cigarette which produces a feeling of success with each light making the attempt to stop smoking even more difficult.

In addition to the disorder of Autism would be the disorders on what they call the Autism spectrum. In other words, Autism with other issues or factors or with an active or inactive Action Thought. These situations that may not be completely Autism are as follows:

1. If the child overcomes the fear and the "me" returns but the fears and talents stay possibly with apprehension.
2. If the "me" does not return but the fear leaves meaning the Thoughts are still ones of disconnect but not with fear.
3. If the "me" returns but not the "you"

The following are situations of loss in Asperger's Syndrome which I believe should still be called Asperger's Syndrome though the DSM-5 has changed it. This makes sense as it is Autism with only a slight lack of understanding another but it really needs to be distinguished since all other aspects of the person's life is working as it should.

1. No loss of the "me" Thought to understand itself but the loss of the "you" Thought though life goes on. They can hold a job, the person would go to work, make money, and maybe have a hobby but would not have a lot of friends. If there is a family involved, the person would be aloof.
2. There is still a loss of the "me" Thought only in relation to the "you" Thought but the person is aware there is something wrong. "Mom, am I an alien?"
3. The person seems like everyone else but they have slight indicators that something is not exactly right and they are not completely like others. They would want a job where they are as solitary as possible and would want to not have to work as a team, they would prefer a house with fewer windows, they would want to be surrounded by something to separate from others like trees, and friendships would have to have a common ground like alcohol or math.

I need to mention here the only healing of severe autism was done by a mother who spent every minute of every day copying the actions of her autistic son until he realized that he was the same as her. That was decades ago.

Garrett Syndrome

Garrett Syndrome is a general term for a missing Thought disorder that happens in a Thought series when the Thought to deactivate a previous Thought is missing. The child lives the Thought until it is replaced but if it is not completely replaced and the Thought is still there it can be used without realizing it should have been retired and replaced.

Garrett Syndrome deals with a multitude of Thoughts that are supposed to be retired and replaced. There are times when the person has no symptoms of Garrett Syndrome and lives a normal life for many years and later show these symptoms. This happens because the Prebirth Thoughts are used after birth and can be part of the person's retrievable memory. Though they had no need to refer to those memories before a trauma when something happens to knock them off their feet, namely remove their leaned upon stability, they remember those Thoughts and not knowing where they came from and why use them unconsciously unknowingly or both.

This is what happened with John Nash and his disorder of Schizophrenia that occurred when he was told his math, which he relied on for his stability, was wrong. It was later proven that he was right but with the belief that he was wrong there was no escape but to backtrack his psyche. The same was true of Sybil. She broke a window to escape but it didn't work so she unconsciously took the same basic route as John Nash.

These Thoughts were used before intentionally retrievable memory was formed so they are unconscious and unknown to the person.

Garrett Syndrome 1:

Prebirth Missing Thought: The loss of the Thought to deactivate a previous Thought to make room for the next Thought.

Prebirth injury: loss of Concept Thought to deactivate previous two-dimensional Thoughts with which the child is born to be replaced with three dimensional objects and possibly object permanence which is the Thought that an object or person still exists even when they are hidden and you can't see or hear them.

Reaction to injury: reliving two dimensional objects and nonobjective sounds, touch, smells, images that were part of the world of the newborn.

Thought group: Truth

Possible connected street name: Schizophrenia, Schizophrenia with hallucinations, Auditory Schizophrenia, Schizotypal

Prebirth and Post Memory Garrett Syndrome 2:

Prebirth Missing Thought: Thought to deactivate Concept to pretend.

Prebirth injury: Loss of the Thought to deactivate previous Thoughts of the imaginary world to make way for new Thoughts of logic and reality.

Reaction to injury: continuing Thought of pretending, lack of self and/or continuity.

Thought group: Truth

Possible connected street name: Schizophrenic delusions, BIID, DID, schizophrenic disorganized Thought

Garrett Syndrome 3:

Prebirth Missing Thought: Thought of trust in logical stability

Post Memory injury: Loss of trust in and use of the current logical foundation, sense of self or continuity with retraction to the pretend stage.

Reaction to injury: reversion to the times and Thought set of pretending, lack of self and/or continuity.

Thought group: Truth

Possible connected street name: Schizophrenic delusions, BIID, DID, schizophrenic disorganized Thought

Garrett Syndrome is a disorder that could be considered to be schizophrenia or on the schizophrenia spectrum. Schizophrenia is a Latin term that means splitting of the mind, because the person's thinking is split between reality and nonreality. Garrett Syndrome is also a split between what we would consider to be reality and nonreality.

Garrett Syndrome is a prebirth disorder that is caused by a loss of Thought before birth that shows up early in children or later in adults. This loss of Thought is the Thought to deactivate a previous Thought to make room for the next Thought, just as a child loses its baby teeth to make room for the adult teeth. If baby teeth are still there when adult teeth come in there is a problem.

In this situation there could be hallucinations that are visual, auditory, tactile, olfactory or gustatory (taste). Auditory hallucinations consist of sounds that would be just sounds, words or sounds with words connected to a visual concept like the vision of a mother. Because the child is at a stage where what is sensed is believed to be real though its world is two dimensional and possibly not object permanent (Piaget discovery), the child will have no doubt in the reality and no doubt of the reality of the later hallucinations. Therefore, activated senses connected to or even not connected to other senses like visual images would be considered real.

In the plan that moves the middle-aged child from a make-believe world to the world of logic there could be a loss of Thought to deactivate the make-believe Thought.

Garrett Syndrome is a rejection of related Thoughts of logical foundational reality that were in the mind preinjury. In other words, Thoughts that are considered the normal state and what fits into what is currently known, accepted or proven to be true are rejected because they are believed to no longer work. The Thought set of logic leaves and is replaced with the previous Thought set of pretending or imagination. The person, when the world of logic lets them down, then regresses back to Thought sets from a previous developmental state that are in memory. Replacement of the logical foundational Thoughts with Thoughts from that previous developmental stage happens.

Due to the fact that Thoughts from the previous developmental stages were believed to be true by the person, the Thoughts from the earlier stage will be believed to be true by the person who is revisiting those memories. This is very important to know.

When we see something, that item we are seeing is not real in our Minds, but a reflection of light. Our eyes turn the image upside down and transmit it to our brains and our brain spins it back the right way…with…every…thing…we…see! And at a speed that is incredible.

Hence, what we think we see is merely a Concept in our Minds. Even though it may be grounded in reality, it is still merely a Concept. There is not a hamburger in someone's head, but an image of one.

Piaget's Sensorimotor Stage:

The set of Thoughts in this stage for the baby is simply for the purpose of learning to use the body in its new world (age birth to two).

At first the baby lives in a two-dimensional world of image, sound and other senses. It starts in a warm place where it doesn't have any clue it has a body. It was swimming untouched in warm water where its world consists of warmth and a bit of jiggling. Then, it is pushed through a canal where it feels for the first time as it is being squeezed, which is how it realizes it has a body. It enters the world with lights flashing, sounds abounding and things touching the new body that it just realized it had.

With the newborn, what the baby first sees are simply pictures to be remembered, since it doesn't have the Thought of depth perception. The things it hears and feels are concepts to be remembered and all these things are stored in memory as such. This image-based thinking is not based in reality as we are not two-dimensional pictures or images. What the baby hears is a sound and that sound may be connected to something or may not, but it is not based on the reality that the sound is coming FROM something instead it would perceive it as just being connected to something. Before the child realizes that the sound is coming from the visual or tactile concept in this earliest stage it hears the sound and either the sound is alone or connects with something in the other senses. This is very important because the fact that this sound is not coming from another thing makes it able to appear any time and be connected to anything the child may think at the time. Just like the visual hallucination the child may connect it to something good or something bad or something with no emotion at all.

These images the baby sees move as the process to see includes the ability, in "The Natural State of Being", to put pictures together to animate the same way it is done in a movie. These images have no material limits, so they can do things that would be physically impossible. This is why hallucinations can fly or just appear and disappear.

The baby lives in an image-based world for months that has been its only world. It has been its deeply believed reality. It knows nothing else. It automatically accepts that this is the real world. This belief that this is the real world is connected to the image-based way of seeing things and the concept-based way of hearing things, meaning just a sense connected to something.

These images feed the baby, hold the baby, are comforting to the baby and make sounds to the baby. The baby can hit the images, push the images, see and hear the images. It can see the actions done by the images and all of this is placed in memory.

Since the baby has not yet learned that the image is something real, permanent and three dimensional, when the object is removed, the baby assumes it is simply gone and moves on to the next thing to look at. When we move from one image that we are looking at to another (which is how we see), the only reason we know that the previous image is there is because we remember it to be there and know it has a permanence. Otherwise, like this baby, we would think the previous image or picture is gone. A coherent story could not be made if each time we see a new image we didn't know the previous one is still there (permanent). All would simply be picture after picture after picture.

When we look out a window and see a tree, we know that tree is an object and has depth and permanence. We don't expect it to simply go away. When we look at a picture on a television screen and the movie ends and the picture fades to black, we accept that the image is gone. We know it has no depth. We know it is only an image, but a baby does not.

The newborn baby does not have the understanding that it lives in the world we live in, namely the solid material world, the world of object permanence and three dimensions.

Later object permanence is activated and the baby suddenly lives in a 3-dimensional world that does not disappear. The first Thought concerning this disorder has to do with object permanence and three-dimensional objects that brings the child from seeing the world as merely pictures with action, like the pictures on the television, to the world of physical or object reality.

Until that Thought is activated, what is seen, heard and touched as real, solid, and three dimensional would simply be seen as an image, heard as a sound, felt as a touch and, most importantly, still believed to be real in that state.

Psychologists who study Jean Piaget believe, as did he, that the appearance of Object Permanence causes a major break in understanding in the baby and that, without this Thought, the objects in the baby's Mind would have no separate, permanent existence. This is true, but I believe the Thought placed through "The Natural State of Being" of three dimensions along with the Thought of Object Permanence is equally as important, as both of these Thoughts show that objects are, in fact, objects and that the objects cannot go through each other, making them real things instead of images as in hallucinations.

The Thought of the Concept of image is fine in memory since television shows are images and pictures on paper are images, but the Thought that an image is real and moves is the Thought that is replaced when the Thought of Object Permanence and three dimensions is activated. If the Thought that images are real is not deactivated, that Thought is still an all-encompassing reality that can activate when it is remembered or needed later on.

A "Task Thought" that is part of "The Natural State of Being" has the job to deactivate the Thought that is connected to the Concept of image, so that it can be properly replaced with the next Thought in the series, which is the Concept of objects and the true reality in three dimensions. Because the "Task Thought" to deactivate the two-dimensional image-based Thought is missing, the Thought concerning images is not removed, but remains active or dormant with the possibility of being unconsciously activated later in the person's life.

The Thought that objects do not go through each other allows the baby to understand that objects rather than images are real. If the two-dimensional image-based Concept Thought that the image is real is not deactivated and replaced with the Object Permanence/three-dimensional Concept, the person will believe that both image-based Concept and Object Permanence/three-dimensional Concept is real for its entire life.

Using objects that have a physical/material base every day prove them to be physically real. However, unconsciously revisiting the image only Thought, because belief in the reality of this Thought is still active when the person is supposed to be completely submersed in the only true reality of Object Permanence/three-dimensions, would cause a psychotic episode or a hallucination. Fear and disequilibrium would also play a part in the situation.

In addition, if the image is there and seems real, why not use it to one's advantage, for example, when the person needs a friend. Homeless people do this all the time to provide themselves with nonthreatening companionship that one would need according to "The Natural State of Being". The option to use the Thought, that should be dormant, allows the person to bounce from reality-based Thoughts of objects that cannot go through each other to image-based Thoughts of objects and do so unconsciously, incidentally and sometimes at will. This is the cause of what many call hallucinations.

When relived in a hallucination, the person unconsciously uses the image-based remembered Thought that is believed to be real, since that image was connected to the belief that it is real and that is all it knew. It is the world of image that the baby believed to be the real world, which makes sense because at that time it had no contrary or opposing Thought of dimensions.

This situation of bouncing from image-based Thoughts to reality-based Thoughts can affect the person's entire life from the beginning causing a childhood illness of schizophrenia. If fear is involved, the "cytokine storm" it would cause would result in extreme behavior in the person, possible fear and possible or probable hyperactivity.

When the child begins to realize that objects cannot move through other objects and that objects don't disappear spontaneously, meaning they have object permanence and three-dimensions, it will understand real physical life.

Garrett Syndrome is a disorder where the image-based Thoughts pertaining to physical reality did not deactivate and the person can or will spontaneously revert back to the Thought where objects are seen as images that do not have a permanence or solidity. These images can move, appear, disappear, make a sound or seem to touch the person, since they do not follow the rules of material law.

The loss of the Concept Thought in the "Task Thought" that deactivates the previous image-based Thought is caused by physical trauma and this trauma can also cause fear, leaving the person with a fear-based hyperactivity in addition to the propensity for hallucinations. This fear can cause a disequilibrium that can cause a flight behavior leading to hand waving and hyperactive behavior meaning behavior to "get rid" of the disequilibrium.

When the child realizes the object is something that has a material basis, since it cannot go through another object and that it stays, the child has stepped into the world of reality. It has also taken its first steps into the world of intelligence, which no one can accurately explain no matter how hard they try and how many psychiatric researchers they read.

Post memory Garrett syndrome

…and the absolutely positively completely separate WORLDS.

It needs to be explained here that there are three different causes of schizophrenia.

> ***The first** cause is the situation where the Concept part of the Task Thought to deactivate the image-based Thought is not placed. This causes hallucinations of all kinds and childhood Schizophrenia. (Birth to object permanence/three dimensions)*

> ***The second** cause is the situation where the Concept part of the Task Thought to deactivate pretending is not placed so that pretending does not shut off but logic is some form does develop. In addition, it is in this stage that the growth of the self and the growth of continuity of Thought develops so that when the person reverts back to this stage the Thought of what the self is and the Thought of continuity can be distorted. (Object permanence/three dimensions to end of pretending)*

> *The **third** cause is the situation of reverting back to a time before object permanence or before the pretending Thought deactivates as in the case of mathematician John Nash who was in the last stage of intellectual development for decades who when he tried to win a prize in math and was rejected making the foundation of his world, to him, inaccurate. He then had a psychotic break where he unconsciously reverted back to the pretending stage thinking he was the Emperor of Antarctica among other things. (It has to be noted here that this third cause is considered a disorder rather than a syndrome because this cause is not from a before birth injury nor does it have a missing Thought). I would consider this a defense mechanism as uncovered by Sigmond Freud.*

No deactivation takes place between the stage where the child realizes the physicality of objects and the intellectual next stage of pretending. The stage of pretending is simply the stage where the child uses what it has learned about its body with the world it lives in. The child, once it has learned to use its body properly, begins to build its Mind with playing and pretending.

The younger child has gone from the image stage to object solidity where the image stage was supposed to deactivate. Next the child simply uses its body by pretending. It then goes from the pretend Thought to logical Thought and in this transition the Thought of pretending is also supposed to deactivate and be replaced with Thoughts of logic.

The child lives in a world that is slowly growing toward logic while keeping what has been learned in memory, which would be Thoughts using pretending. What it has learned in the pretending stage will be used in the last stage of development to learn abstract things like religion. The next stage of intellectual growth after pretending, the logic stage, is activated, and pretending is deactivated. It is the realization or the activation of the Thought that what was before may not be real at all that changes everything and logic takes over.

Hence, the two worlds. In one world is the set of Thoughts that are representational and believed as real and the other is what is actually real. And these worlds do not mix. In other words, a person cannot be mentally a child and mentally an adult at the same time. It's one or the other.

The last situation happens in the world of logic and abstract Thought. It is the world of the normal average adult. A person anywhere beyond the stage of pretending can regress to the pretend stage if trauma causes it to search elsewhere for answers it needs to go back to equalization.

One world is learning what is real and what is not through object representation and the other one logically knows what is real and what is not. It is the representation of one thing for another and the still active belief in the reality of representation that leads to the delusions. By using the Thoughts in "The Natural State of Being" younger children will automatically use one thing to represent another and believe in the world where that can be and is done like Santa coming down the chimney. This unconscious behavior is what takes over the person with delusions when they regress since for the person two plus two no longer equals four and therefore, can equal anything and everything else.

The first world of image only Thoughts gives way to the next world of object permanence and three dimensions or the Thoughts of reality of objects. This is done in Piaget's Preoperational stage. The Thoughts in this stage deal with what is representational in relation to objects.

Preoperational Thought deals with objects with Thought and Concrete Operational Thought deals with Thought with objects. It is a switch in sequence. There is a complete realization that pretending is pretending and that the world of pretending is not real.

In the pretending stage, the make-believe world the child lives in where it hasn't learned to put together facts to make a conclusion is a make-believe world and it is EVERYTHING. There is no other world to the child. This make-believe world is again EVERYTHING absolutely EVERYTHING… the whole universe to the child. The world of the child in this set of Thoughts includes no formal logic. MAKE BELIEVE WITH OBJECTS IS GENERAL AND IT IS ALL…EVERYTHING.

It is in this world in which the child lives that the child learns things like the existence of the self and continuity as well as the representation of one thing for another. This makes the person who retreats back to this time very vulnerable.

To emphasize this separation of worlds we can do an experiment. Sit with a five-year-old child who is playing with dolls or trucks and see how long you can last as an adult. See how hard it is to actually get as mentally involved in the child's play as the child is. You can physically play,

129

but to mentally play as the child would play would not be real. It is this deeply believed world of pretend that is supposed to later on deactivate that does not deactivate.

The problem in Garrett Syndrome that occurs after retrievable memory is formed makes perfect sense. Psychologists can attest to the fact that most (and I would say all) of the people who suffer from schizophrenic delusions suffered some sort of trauma. This trauma would be in the person who uses formal thinking or the ability to put together facts to make a conclusion. If all of the "facts" the person uses do not work and it is unable to "put together facts to make a conclusion", the person, pushed by the Action Thought, and disequilibrium, will unconsciously search another place for the needed answers. And where else could they search, but the previous set of Thoughts that are already placed in memory AND BELIEVED TO BE TRUE? In other words, they regress to the former set of Thoughts that include make believe and/or hallucinations.

The first set of Thoughts concerning Schizophrenia deals with the things spoken of in Piaget's Sensorimotor stage. The second set of Thoughts consist of things presented in Piaget's Preoperational and Concrete Operational stages. The third set of Thoughts consists of the Thoughts in the logical world, in the Concrete Operational stage and Formal Operational stage which is where all adults who have had no injury live. It is from this stage of logic that the person, due to a stressful or traumatic situation, would leave the world of logic and revert back to previous Thought or Thoughts that are illogical and make believe.

These three basic sets of Thoughts make what would be considered to be the structural foundation of reality-based Thought in the child. The purpose of this last set of Thoughts is to "think" in relation to the real world. These reality-based Thoughts are in addition to the natural progression of physical and cognitive growth.

The second section of reality-based Thoughts would consist of the Thoughts of imagination first with physical logic-based Thoughts second slowly changing to logical thinking with imagination second. The pretending part or childlike imagination deactivates once what was learned from it is placed in memory. Then logical thinking first with imagination second activates and stays for the person's life. What is in memory is always remembered and used when necessary, but the person is no longer in need of practicing with it and moves on to the last Thought that teaches for a lifetime.

It is in this set of Thoughts that the person can understand abstract ideas that have no physical reference like love, beauty, freedom, morality and so on. It is no longer limited to what is physically seen and heard.

The Thoughts in the third set are of logic (the formal principals of reason) along with representational imagination. The person is logical, but its Mind uses that logic with imagination. This person has the ability to use nonphysical Concepts, which as an adult would relate to things like Love. This Thought that continues to grow from age twelve to adulthood, is the final set of Thoughts concerning intellectual and reality-based Thoughts and has no "Task Thought" attached for it to deactivate. This Thought set is present in the person with no issues who is able to use the Thought of logic with the Thought of imagination which is the way the world works for the uninjured adult.

A deeper developmental look or an awkward chronology:

The child that was born into an image-based world had not yet learned object permanence or three dimensions. By the time it got to the second set of reality-based Thoughts, the child had been in the world for only two years or so. Everything is still centered around its self. When it cried, someone came by to fix the problem. When it ate, someone was there looking it in the eye and placing food in its mouth. People would look at it and make funny faces and noises. There is so much it still hasn't learned. Previously, it saw this animated thing in front of it that can move and is connected to sounds. If it saw a ball, a bug or butterfly go by in the air it may think that all things can fly. Why wouldn't it think that? Well, until, of course, it fell down. It is programmed to continually play with its new body and does so incessantly. It still sees things from its own point of view because it hadn't yet learned otherwise. There is only so much it can learn and there is so much to be learned and it's still building its "self".

Trial and error teach the basic skills of how to use the body in the Sensorimotor stage, where the plan for learning has accomplished its goal and taught all that is needed according to "The Natural State of Being". These Thoughts or learned concepts are all placed in memory.

The child, in this stage, believes almost everything is alive as much as it knows of what alive is. It believes the sun is alive because it believes that what moves is alive and it perceives the sun to move up and down in the sky and it believes it follows them. Since "things are alive because they move" is in its face all day long, why wouldn't it believe images are real? It believes that all things are alive along with many other childlike untrue beliefs.

The types of Thoughts in this time of development and in this syndrome present as reality because they relate to what the person completely believes to be real and the only thing it knows to be true.

More commonly known disorders:

Psychotic breaks: Psychotic breaks happen later in life and mostly cause delusions, though some also have hallucinations as well depending on how far back the Mind goes for the answer it desperately seeks. Most if not all situations concerning psychotic breaks where the person is not drugged or mentally or physically injured happen during stressful situations where the Mind tries to get desperately needed answers.

Thoughts that did not deactivate can stay dormant for a lifetime and can be completely unknown to the person. Often those with schizophrenia will say they had a trigger. The trigger is usually not from physical trauma but mental. A mental situation that is very pressing and can only be solved with thinking, according to the person, causes the person to search its Mind for the unachievable answer. When all they know fails the Mind searches more and inadvertently searches beyond the world it knows namely into the past. This activates the memory of the previously lived Thought and the person mentally leaves the current set of Thoughts it lives in for the ones in the past that did not deactivate.

In the case of John Nash, he tried and tried to do and learn what was needed to win the award he so coveted not realizing the answer he had was correct all along. This situation of being told he was wrong left him nowhere to go. The search in his Mind for the answer led him to the Thoughts in the world of pretend causing delusions like the delusion that he was "the emperor of Antarctica". After years of being hurt by this situation he finally was healed or better said the pretend Thought was deactivated. It also helped that the math problem that caused him to be thrown off was later realized to be done correctly by him so two plus two equaled four again.

Another young man who suddenly developed schizophrenia was also very intelligent. He was going to high school and college in Mexico at the same time and was under enormous pressure. His delusions were helped with medication and family and friends who were there for him.

Memories start sometime before we are born. Though not purposely retrievable they are there to teach us throughout our lives. Recall may not work but memories do not leave.

The adult who reverts back to memories that were dormant and still hold image-based Thoughts later in their life will suffer from hallucinations. An adult who regresses back to a Thought from the world of pretend will suffer from delusions. For family and the person there is confusion and fear. Parents of children in this situation and family of adults in this situation are thrown into the world of psychiatrics and medicine that is a huge pool of mud in which everyone is drowning as they attempt to save their loved one. It is heartbreaking.

In the adult, and sometimes the child, this situation can be a coping mechanism. "The Natural State of Being" is for the person to be social and have friends. With the child or adult who lives in a world that switches realities, there are few who have friends who will understand.

This often causes the person to use the images of friends to fill social needs that are part of "The Natural State of Being" and this is done with hallucinations rather than the person trying to fill social needs with someone they cannot understand who lived a normal life with no hallucinations and who cannot understand them.

A reversion back to a good memory as well as one that unconsciously relates to stability, warmth and security is why the homeless man talks to and even argues with imaginary people. This action fulfills the social need in "The Natural State of Being" without causing real stress. The person understands the imagined person because it is their own idea.

Someone once said that to remove the stimming of a person with Autism was cruel. Removing the only way that a person with a disability such as this can fulfill the need for social interaction according to "The Natural State of Being" may be cruel as well.

In the story and healing of Sybil, Dr. Wilbur already replaced the need for social interaction by loving Sybil as a mother for eleven years and giving her back her one and only self. The need was filled first.

In the case of Trudy Chase, also known as "Trudy and the Troops", though Trudy had multiple personality disorder like Sybil (today known as dissociative identity disorder), she had no substitute for the illusionary friendships. Even though she knew they were not real she decided to keep them throughout her life and not heal.

With adults and some children there isn't always a pure reversion back. There is often baggage that can be part of the hallucination. They go back to that memory, but add the experiences of their world to it like fear of a scary clown or vicious cat.

Some hallucinations are thought to whisper to the person that they are bad people. One person's image/concept hallucination presented as a clown from the movie "It" and another time presented as a little girl who was holding a knife. The stabbing with the imaginary knife would feel as painful as the stabbing with a real knife though it is not real. It would be a memory or a memory of how that would feel in real life. Also, the person can get real stab wounds if they unconsciously stab themselves.

By time the person reaches the second set, assuming nothing has gone wrong, the Concept that the object is permanent has already been activated. Eventually as the baby plays with objects, knowing that the object that is out of sight is still there another Thought is activated. If that object is still there everything must be there as well including...its physical self.

When the Thought Concept of the self-activates it becomes a real concept to the child as a whole. The single concept of the existence of "the self" is one Thought. It is the general Thought of "the self" and it is the same for everyone. But aspects and characteristics of the self are activating bit by bit as well. The self is being built while the fantasy and representational Thought is still at work. This is why children play dress up with fancy dresses or frog boots or even footballs as a prop for their personality.

But there are two parts to this situation. The child not only has the Thought activated that it has an individual "self" but it has another Thought that has to be activated and that Thought is of the separation of the newly realized "self" from the environment and the existence of the environment as its own Concept.

When there are disorders, like when fantasy magical pretend Thoughts do not deactivate, the Thoughts get mixed up and, though it sometimes affects the whole self and sometimes does not affect the whole self, it can cause horrendous problems. It is here that the person's self or concept of self could be distorted.

Below are just a few of the huge numbers of situations where the self and the fantasy that is believed to be real is mixed and the mixed Thought is placed in memory.

At the same time the individual and personal characteristics of self of the child are slowly and methodically being activated piece by piece in conjunction with the stages of development and "The Natural State of Being".

If the child becomes aware of itself as a self, and lives in and believes in fantasies the child may mix the two concepts and believe it is the actual object of the fantasy which is fine for a child but logic will set in and the child will realize eventually that is not true unless the Thought to deactivate the fantasy pretend Thought does not happen.

Since the child lives in the pretend and logical world at the same time it can attach to something that is not real and that Thought will stay. What the child has attached to is individual and could be animate or inanimate and since pretend can override logic due to guilt or desire the fantasy Thought will stay.

The concept in the Mind of the child includes its self and eventually includes the object universe in which it lives, the universe as permanence and the universe as a whole. If there is a problem with the self as a concept with object permanence and/or the concept of the environment as an object of permanence in relation to the self and the Thought that distinguishes them is missing the person can have a missing sense of self and/or a missing sense of its self in the world. (depersonalization/derealization).

If the child sees something that makes no sense or produces guilt like, for instance, seeing someone who is blind and they are not blind it may also cause a disequilibrium the person would desperately need to fix. The Thought then gets placed in memory and though other Thoughts may work fine, this one that was placed in memory without logic using pretend may remain until changed. This would account for the person later in life being obsessed with becoming blind in order to even things out or make things right.

The woman who thinks she is a lion and has gotten very expensive plastic surgery to look like a lion believes she is a lion. If logic does not win over the fantasy Thought, which it usually does, the person will believe with all their heart in the fantasy as being who they are. They may believe they are a wolf or a lion or that someone else is a particular animal, again, because the Thought from the time of fantasy did not get replaced with logic and is still in memory and believed. (Lycanthropy). It is curious that no one has as of yet said they were a dung beetle or a maggot but who knows!

Objectophiles are those who fall in love with inanimate objects like their car or like the person who married the Eiffel Tower or the Berlin Wall. There is a woman who fell in love with the statue of the Greek God Adonis. One woman from the age of 13 was in love with the 1001 Nachts ride at the fair ground. At age 12 a boy fell in love with a Hammond Organ which he has since left for a steam locomotive. Yes, those are real. They also show the age of the onset of the disorder. For these people, the Thought to deactivate the pretend Thought did not happen.

There is species dysphoria where a person thinks they are another species. There is another type of this situation called Transspeciesism for those who think they are only partially human. There is Delusional Misidentification Syndrome where the person thinks they are physically changing into a different identity. Therians are ones who think they have a strong spiritual or mental connection to an animal. Theriaanthropy is where the person thinks they have the ability to metamorphose into other animals by means of shapeshifting. Bronies which is when a person, mostly males, has a fascination with My Little Pony.

These are rare as the logic of it would probably win over the fantasy before the Thought is placed in memory and does so in most cases.

There are situations where the person believes they have too many legs or needs to be blinded because they are not comfortable with their eyes. This can happen when there is a trauma or inequality seen by the child at the time when the child is going through the process of building the self. If there is an unconscious feeling of guilt when the bodily situation of another is observed, when the child sees an unfairness that causes a problem with equilibrium the child could desire to remove a limb or eyes to make the situation equal. If there is an unusual objectivity like a horse having four legs and a person having two the very young child could mix the concepts and think they should have three legs. (BIID) This Thought would leave with logic unless the Thought to deactivate pretend Thought was not placed.

There is a situation where the person believes a 5-year-old is in love with them or a movie star is in love with them. This is the same disorder.

There is a situation where the person believes they are other people and usually more than one other person. This is known to be something that happens before the child is four years old due to a trauma of fear or guilt or both. (Dissociative Identity Disorder). In the case of Shirley Ann Mason better known as Sybil the situation was kept in order to survive. In the case of Trudy Chase, the situation was kept purposefully for her whole life.

The concept of transgender may be one of the Thoughts in this situation as well provided it was not a learned thing or an actual physical abnormality. (gender dysphoria).

Schizophreniform: This type of schizophrenia lasts 4 to 6 months. In this situation the person reverts back to the second set of Thoughts but there is no missing Thought. Trauma is probably the trigger and makes the person look for an answer in a place other than the in the set logical Thoughts where they had been mentally living. The use of the second set of Thoughts in no longer believed or needed and the person goes back to a set of Thoughts of the current time.

Schizoid: This is not a schizophrenic disorder but it is a lost Thought disorder.

Undifferentiated schizophrenia is to have two types of schizophrenia or more of delusions, hallucinations, disorganized speech or behavior or catatonic behavior.

Schizoaffective: schizophrenia with mood disorder or fear that causes the Action Thought to fight back causing depression.

Disorganized Thinking: Often fear is a part of this situation and plays a very big role. Here the person bounces quickly from the second Thought that did not deactivate to the third because of the actions of the Action Thought. This bouncing may also be with the other Thoughts as well. Fear would need to be relieved in this disorder as it plays a huge role because the person does not understand what is going on.

Catatonic Schizophrenia: The program of the Mind shuts down just like a computer from data overload. In the older computers pressing a button too fast over and over would result in a crash that required a reboot. This is the same situation where the person is caught between two sets of Thoughts and simply doesn't or can't choose either.

The action Thought in these disorders is very strong. It is strong enough for a person to put lye in their eyes to go blind and put their feet in dry ice to destroy the skin and cause amputation. These disorders may be weird and unusual but they are very real and destructive.

If there is no missing Thought it is still possible for the person to revert back to a previous stage of development because of trauma. When this happens, it is sometimes impossible to tell if there was a loss of Thought before birth or if the reversion is just a way to cope. If the reversion is a coping mechanism the person would have a disorder as opposed to Garrett Syndrome.

The problem in relation to Prebirth Garrett Syndrome is not a problem with imagination since imagination is part of "The Natural State of Being" but the loss of the Thought to deactivate not the Thoughts in this second section but the belief of them being real (schizotypal disorder) The problem in relation Post Memory Garrett Syndrome is not a problem of imagination either but the reversion back to this second set and the Thought that what is in the remembered Thoughts are real (delusional schizophrenia). The problem for those who regress to or stay in this set of Thoughts is that at the time the memories were made the child believed with every part of its mind that what it thinks is real and true. Going back in time would be no problem if it were not believed to be true.

If nothing goes wrong, at the appropriate time the "Task Thought" to deactivate the Thought of magical illogical representational thinking being completely true will activate. Logic and reason will eventually override fantasy and fantasy and magical thinking will stop but the ability to imagine continues even later into religion or invention. Without imagination we would not progress past what is materially obvious and would not believe in any nonmaterial thing like religion.

For those with this syndrome the fun and empowerment make it something they may not want to end and some will want to keep their magical thinking all of their lives. But they should still understand why it is happening.

If there are hallucinations at this time as well due to the lack of deactivation the first Thought, the hallucinations will also be part of the beliefs of the person. The person may believe the hallucinations to be real or if it is a very intelligent person realize the hallucinations are not exactly like other object permanent 3-dimensional people, animals or whatever. They may name the hallucinations at this time a name different from say a cat that they have that is real or a real person like Fluffy or Jane for instance. They may use these hallucinations with the continued belief in what they call "magical thinking" and seem more away from reality than they actually are.

If there is an injury and the Concept Thought in the "Task Thought" to deactivate the Thought that what is imagined and unreal is not there, the Action Thought to activate the "Task Thought" may begin to push to do its job and cause disequilibrium. This in turn causes sadness or depression as disequilibrium often does and is supposed to do. The Action Thought may relax and the person may go back in their magical world only to activate again causing disequilibrium again and the situation repeats or the Action Thought may relax and the person is in the world of what is real only for the unreal Thoughts to start up again. This situation causes confusion, a separation from the rest of the world.

One man who has this disorder said that he can't understand why, as a grown man, he has the strongest desire to hug a teddy bear and actually does so. Imagine the emotional toll that takes. But for someone who understands this disorder the fact that he would want to hug a teddy bear would be nothing unusual.

In trying to make sense of what it is seeing and hearing the Mind fills in the gaps by making the picture look real as it does with a movie since that is logically what should be and what it sees and hears would have attributes of what would really be. For instance, an image of a cat would be given the ability to act as a cat. The sound of a voice would be able to say human sounding things because the Mind is trying to make sense of things. If the person is upset with themselves or another person the sound will say things that are bad if the person wants to do something the sound will say something that allows the person to do a particular bad act.

The Mind trying to make sense of things happens all day long and can be exhausting and depressing.

Denning Syndrome

    Prebirth Missing Thought: Various Thoughts dealing with learning
    Prebirth injury: Loss of Concept, Action Thought or complete Task Thoughts related to learning
    Reaction to injury: loss of cognitive ability
    Kind of Thought: Truth
    Possible connected street name: cognitive or intellectual disabilities (formerly mental retardation)

If you were to be fair and loving to all people you would make them basically the same intelligence with the ability to use the skills of intelligence needed in daily life. You certainly wouldn't make some lower than others.

There are many influences that determine what a person will learn in their life. They are the school system, parental influence, life circumstances, preferences in time spent, etc.

There are also many Concepts that are part of the learning system in the human being. They are, of course, part of "The Natural State of Being" and are planted in the child before birth.

The former common term for the situation where a person is unable to cognitively do what others their age can do is mental retardation which I consider to be a vulgar and demeaning term to describe those with cognitive disabilities. In addition, it is completely inaccurate and indicates that the person simply needs to speed up as the term retard from the word ritardando which is Italian and means slow. The truth is that they are not thinking slowly, but in reality, are completely stopped.

There are more terms that are or were used to describe those with cognitive disabilities which, though still demeaning, show a relationship to the stages of development discovered by Jean Piaget. This, to me, is quite telling and supports the accuracy of the stages published by Piaget. The old term for a person at the Sensorimotor stage would be idiot. The old term for a person at the Preoperational stage would be imbecile. The old term for a person at a later stage would be moron. This is to say that people with no knowledge of development or Piaget were able to recognize the difference in those with cognitive disabilities and categorize them even though it was done not very nicely.

The one reason and probably the most common one concerning cognitive disabilities has to do with the Thoughts from "The Natural State of Being" that were supposed to have been placed to be activated at a particular time in any of the Sensorimotor, Preoperational, Concrete Operational and Formal Operational developmental stages. One example would be the Thought of

Assimilation or lack thereof. Another example would be the Thought of Accommodation or lack thereof.

Assimilation is the most basic learning Thought placed in the child and probably the first to be activated. From the very start this "Task Thought" is activated and used by the baby probably before its birth and certainly directly after its birth. It is simply the cognitive process by which we take in information and place it in memory.

If the Concept Thought is missing the child can do nothing. If the Action Thought is missing or damaged the child can learn by rote with a lesson being repeated over and over. The use of Assimilation may allow the person to learn by rote if the Action Thought is missing causing the lack of purposeful placement in memory. A person who could only learn from Assimilation by rote would have a low IQ or no measurable IQ.

Accommodation allows the person's Mind to alter what they already know to accommodate new information into a new Thought to be placed in memory. These Thoughts would be used with the child in the sensorimotor stage and thereafter. A person who does not have the Thought of Accommodation would not be able to learn but can put things in memory that were introduced by experience without being able to change its Mind.

The process of being able to hold a Thought while placing another and then holding that Thought allows a person to read using phonics. If the ability to hold a Thought while adding another is not functioning properly the person would only be able to learn to read using memorized sight words with repetition. It may be correct to state here that a factor in the IQ of the person would be the ability to hold a Thought while placing another Thought and the general ability to remember. Chess players have a great ability to do this.

After the ability to use Assimilation and Accommodation, the question then is which Thought of the hundreds or thousands introduced to the child that would be used to grow would be activated and would remain inactive due to injury.

In the Thoughts to be activated, for example, if Assimilation and Accommodation were working as they should, and no other Thought is missing the child would progress mostly as planned through the stages of development.

The following will give you an idea of the things some children cannot do if a Thought that would normally be activated is not activated due to lack of placement. Each Thought Concept is placed through "The Natural State of Being" and each has a timer that is to activate at the right time in the right sequence. If any of the Thoughts that are of major importance are missing the child cannot move on to the next stage.

Stuck in the Sensorimotor stage
A person who did not have the Thoughts needed to move on to the Preoperational stage due to a loss of a particular Thought before birth would stay in the Sensorimotor stage and continue through life with an IQ of about 0-26. For example, a person would be stuck in this stage if the

Thought was not placed to be later activated at the right time to realize words and objects can be symbols for something else.

Stuck in the Preoperational stage

A person who did not move on to the Concrete Operational stage due to a loss of Thought before birth would stay in the Preoperational stage and continue through life with an IQ of about 26-50. If, for example, the Concept of thinking in connection to physical objects and physical laws is not placed sometime during this time of its life this child will not move on. If this child does not have the Concept that it can mentally manipulate information it will stay in this stage.

Stuck in the Concrete Operational stage

A person who did not move on to the Formal Operational stage due to a loss of Thought before birth would stay in the Concrete Operational stage and continue through life with an IQ of about 50-70. The Concept of using rules would have been placed but those rules would have to be linked to something physical. This stage has many Concepts that are placed. Each one has a degree of importance.

The Thought of abstract thinking is supposed to be placed and activated in the last stage which is the Formal Operational stage. If the Concept of abstract thinking is not placed to be activated sometime between age twelve and adulthood in the child's life, the child would be considered to be "slow", meaning it will not move on to be the complete adult it was planned to be. The child, however, is not slow but stopped.

I have given you an example of Thoughts in each of the stages that would have caused severe disabilities if they were not placed in the Mind of the child. But the number of Thoughts that can cause both major and minor problems is tremendous and what they all are is currently unknown.

Though the above scenario explains this disorder best there are a few other reasons for this disorder. One deals with memory. One deals with the ability to hold a Thought while processing another. One deals with the speed of Thought that may be an issue as well which I will discuss later.

If a person has memory issues it wouldn't be because of an unplanted Thought. It would be due to physical brain issues which would not be the topic here. The situation where one has to hold a Thought while processing another and do so repeatedly is what it takes to read using phonics and decoding. Being able to do this supremely is what separates us from the Bobby Fisher chess players of the world. Can this be taught? Possibly.

The speed of Thought was somewhat of a mystery. The speed of Thought dealing with things already learned and practiced can be incredibly fast since that would be needed for walking and talking and drinking especially if one is doing all at the same time. This can be accomplished because the child is simply recalling something already in memory, maybe with a little remembered adjustment.

But the speed of Thought in trying to figure out what to do in a new situation is a different story. And for some it may include trying to use a Thought that is not there. You can sometimes see the fear in someone's face when that situation occurs. If there are any brain issues the number of lost Thoughts would be or could be unknown. This would make the person seem to be not very intelligent or actually not be intelligent.

The inability to use memory would actually be the inability to use the Thought of automatic recall. The inability to recall could be influenced by experiences and recall can be forced to a point. If the Thought to consciously recall is not there the person could learn by rote or repetition by continually placing the Thought to be recalled in the person's experience. The Thought to use recall could be considered to be forced but this does not cause stress and works well at times.

If there is no ability to use Assimilation and Accommodation there would be no memory because the Thoughts to place what is learned in memory is not present. Therefore, there would be no memory available for use with other Thoughts. And needless to say, the person would learn nothing. The person would sit in a chair and do nothing of its own accord. I know children like this.

Piaget wrote extensively on the subject of intelligence though not in the context of a missing Thought being the cause of low intelligence. His work is very valuable and should be read in relation to this subject if you want to continue to understand cognition.

Needless to say, this topic is very complex but the loss of any Thought that is dealing with cognition no matter what Thought it is will probably become a problem for the person.

Robinson Syndrome

    Prebirth Missing Thought: Receiving happiness
    Prebirth injury: loss if the Concept Thought of receiving happiness with no drive from the Action Thought
    Reaction to injury: the inability to feel happy, melancholy feeling
    Kind of Thought: Life
    Possible connected street name: Schizoid

When the Concept of happiness is missing and the Action Thought is not active the person will not feel any drive but will just know something is missing and be sad. There would be an emptiness with no drive to replace the emptiness with happiness but the person may not know what is missing. It would be that others are different but the person is not suffering.

Because the missing Concept concerns happiness and the Action Thought is not pushing for happiness the person will not feel the loss.

Mallor Syndrome

    Prebirth Missing Thought: Receiving happiness
    Prebirth injury: Loss if the Concept Thought of receiving happiness with a drive from the Action Thought
    Reaction to injury: the inability to feel happy with the drive to push to feel happy
    Kind of Thought: Life
    Possible connected street name: Clinical Depression (as a mental disorder)

When the Concept of happiness is missing and the Action Thought is active the person will feel a drive the same as the drive in Bennett Syndrome. There would be an emptiness with a drive to replace the emptiness with happiness but the person would have no idea how to do that.

Because the missing Concept concerns happiness and the Action Thought is pushing for happiness the person will feel the loss and become depressed. The depression will stay with its impact depending on the power of the Action Thought. What role Equilibrium plays is unknown.

Jansen Syndrome

> **Prebirth Missing Thought:** Thought of stability connected to being safe with overactive Action Thought
> **Prebirth injury:** loss if the concept of stability with Action Thought activity possibly caused by spontaneous fear
> **Reaction to injury:** attempt to go back to equilibrium causes bouncing from depression from disequilibrium to extreme happiness and back as the Acton Thought attempts to return to a state of equalization.
> **Kind of Thought:** Love
> **Possible connected street name:** Bipolar Disorder

It is the study of this situation that brought about the understanding that the Action Thought acts at various times and in varying degrees.

This was the hardest disorder to study. People with this disorder tend to discuss only the bounce from depression to mania and back with no discussion of the actual cause of the bouncing. I did find one story where the person talks about the onset of bipolar disorder coming from seeing a dead body floating next to the canoe that she was in. This would make fear and spontaneous and severe lack of safety the cause. The situation in which this fear happened can be completely unknown to the person and it is possible they have no memory of it.

An extreme and spontaneous fear can cause a reversion to the pretend Thought set similar to the one that caused the reversion in schizophrenia. This reversion would be the first manic episode. Since extreme fear caused the reversion in the first place that fear would probably still be part of the Thought in the first manic episode. This extreme fear, that may not be felt as fear, along with the reversion to the pretend set of Thoughts would cause confusion and disequilibrium.

The pretend Thought set is fun and away from the logic Thought set that contained the fear that started the whole thing. There would be an unconscious desire to stay in the manic state where the pretend Thoughts are safer. The pretend part of the manic state may be desirable especially since the prior stability in the logic set of Thoughts is believed to be unable to protect the person. But the person can't stay in this pretend Thought set forever since the Action Thought would be fighting to remove confusion and disequilibrium and logic would be fighting to return as well. Therefore, because of the Action Thought there would be an unconscious push to leave the manic state and since this state is fun and seems safer there would be a desire to stay at the same time.

The Action Thought is part of the "Task Thought" whose job it is in this situation to keep things logically stable. This Action Thought will fight the confusion and disequilibrium to try to get

147

back to the state of logical Thought before the fear causes all the chaos. In its drive to expel the person from their world of pretending to stop the confusion and disequilibrium and get the person back to the world of logic the Action Thought powerfully rejects the pretend world.

The Action Thought pushes the person out of the illogical manic state of confusion causing the person to no longer have the safety of the pretend Thought set. The confusion is still there as is the disequilibrium, fear and perceived lack of safety. This fearful confused state leads to the person unconsciously searching for another safe haven. But there is none but the worlds of logic where the safety was removed or pretend. Therefore, the person goes into a depression.

It needs to be mentioned here that the stigma of mental illness and instability of not understanding what ones Mind is doing adds a tremendous weight to the whole situation. No one who is and has always been mentally stable can understand what it would be like to suddenly lose the mental ground that one has always relied upon.

After being tossed out of the world of pretend the person will either go into the world that we all live in or directly into a depression. Since the spontaneous unconscious fear that cause this whole scenario is still there the person will go back into a depression eventually even though there may be some time between the mania and depression.

At this time the Action Thought tries to push the person out of the depression not because it should be out of the depression but because the job of the "Task Thought" is still as it was before to secure the person in a logically stable world.

The Action Thought is not predictable. It can be very strong or weak. It can activate at any time and last for any length of time throwing the person into a state of going from depression to mania or depression to normalcy to mania and back again and do so rapidly or slowly and anything in between.

The person at this point then ends up back in the manic pretend Thought set and the cycle starts again.

Of course, with any mental situation the person could have the feelings of anger, fear, the desire to be away from people, jealousy of those not ill and a whole host of other typically human emotions.

Disequalization Syndrome or Disorder:

> **Missing prebirth or post birth Thought: the Thought of applying equalization to all aspects of life.**
> **Injury: Loss of the Thought discomfort from that which is fundamentally untrue**
> **Reaction to injury: floundering through life, instability, denial of basic truths or a basic truth**
> **Thought group: Love/Truth**
> **Possible connected street name: None**

The state of equilibrium is a condition of being where what is true resides. We are made as our natural stare of being to seek truth which is based on love in the workings of our Mind. When something goes wrong as in the situation of learning and Accommodation for example the Mind fights to return to this state of being which includes and is based on truth that reflects growth and love. This return to what is correct is done on the larger scale and the smaller scale within Task Thoughts.

If the Thought of Equilibrium is not active in the Mind the child will not grow. Because we are loved we have Equilibrium, because we have Equilibrium, we grow. Equilibrium concerning learning in the Mind is either there or it is not. The state of Equilibrium in the works of the unseen and minute Thoughts in the Mind are not subject to change. It is not conscious.

But the Thought of equilibrium is not just for smaller unconscious intricate things like learning. It is a Thought that pertains to much more. In many ways we have gotten away from this equal natural loving truthful state when dealing with life but are able to return to it at will. At will is the operant term for some. If the Thought of what would make us equal and our world equal like fairness and love is not in the child's Mind concerning the world it will not be able to change leaving it to flounder through life. If the person is able to change but decides not to for whatever reason it will not change,

Equilibrium is part of "The Natural State of Being" that says something is wrong and is similar to a fever in the body. This disequilibrium might cause both mentally and physically running away behavior or what could be called hyperactivity. But in order to say something is wrong one has to have as a foundation of Truth and Love and a desire for what is true and right.

Chapter 15
Post Birth Thought Disorders

These Thoughts are Thoughts that happened after birth. I call them Life Acquired Thoughts because they happened from experiences as the person lives their life. The Thought that causes the illness called PTSD is a post birth Life Acquired Thought and is considered to be a mental illness. Thought sets that are called Personality Disorders may be post birth Life Acquired Thoughts or they may be prebirth Thoughts. The reason they are considered post birth Life Acquired Thoughts is that the Concept Thought is intact.

Thoughts that cause Schizophrenia, Multiple Personality Disorder, Gender Dysphoria Disorder and possibly Bipolar Disorder are also Life Acquired Thoughts but they often cause the person to lose a prebirth Thought that is a Concept Thought. In reality, it is hard sometimes to say if some disorders are post birth Life Acquired Thoughts or prebirth syndromes or both.

Since Concept Thoughts are flooding into the child's Mind before it is born along with their Action Thoughts it is hard to tell whether a prebirth loss played a part in a post birth disorder.

If there is no "concept" loss the problem has to be in the Action Thought. This means the person does not have to replace a Thought that is missing of which they have no knowledge or memory but they have to remove or slow down or replace an "action". This is true of phobias as well.

Similar to Assimilation and Accommodation one is adjusting and the other is adding. Thoughts that need the "Action Thought" to change are different from Thoughts that require a concept to be placed because it is not there. Each one has an effect on a Thought from "The Natural State of Being" whether it is peace or Love or concept or whatever, it needs fixing. When the loss or change took place, whether it was before birth or after birth, may be common sense or it may not.

Illnesses that are caused by an injury to a Thought before birth are called Syndromes in this book. They would require knowing what the concept from "The Natural State of Being" that should be in the Concept Thought would be in order to replace it. Illnesses that happen after birth to a Thought are called disorders in this book. They would require knowing what the action from "The Natural State of Being" that it should be doing in the Action Thought but are not in order to adjust it.

Injuries to a Thought after birth can happen as well as injuries before birth and they can also cause a missing part of a Thought or a missing Thought entirely. Once the baby is born and all is working as it should it can suffer a physical injury that can cause the loss of either Concept Thought, Action Thought or both. This would typically be called a TBI or Traumatic Brain Injury.

Thoughts that happen before birth are not influenced by post birth environment, people or choice as Thoughts after birth would be. The syndromes before birth are from a Thought that is unknowingly, unconsciously missing. The same cannot be said of post birth Thought disorders.

If there is no physical trauma or medical condition the person can still have a mental illness. Loss of a Concept Thought is not common in mental illnesses that happen after birth and would not happen for no reason.

But after a child is born, loss of an Action Thought or inactivity of an Action Thought is very possible. It seems that post birth Action Thoughts can be completely stopped with no conscious Thought of it happening. (I know of two children who were thrown against a wall at a young age who had their intellectual growth stop at that very moment). It can also be stopped due to a choice made by the person whether they realize what their choice is doing or not.

Healing a post birth inactive Action Thought would require realization of the Thought, since it is a logical Thought that others have that would be obvious to the average person   It would also require a desire to understand. The sufferer doesn't always choose to heal when there is an Action Thought that is inactive and may have consciously or unconsciously made the Thought inactive.

It needs to be stated that many disorders that happen after the child is born deal with Life Acquired Thoughts that are more obvious.

Laughton Disorder

Missing or inactive Action Thought: Loss or inactivity of an Action Thought concerning the personal self and one or more of its fundamental traits from "The Natural State of Being".
Injury: Loss of use of a Concept from "The Natural State of Being" due to Inactivity of an Action Thought having to do with the personal self and its traits that would be in "The Natural State of Being".
Reaction to injury: inability to behave as one with all the general fundamental personality traits that are in "The Natural State of Being".
Thought group: Truth or Love
Possible connected street name: Personality Disorders

This disorder manifests in different ways depending on the particular trait that is inactive. It is with the person all the time and does not involve a trigger to make it active. All types of disorders in this illness have in common that the behaviors in this disorder are not triggered by any incident when they are acted out. The behaviors of those with this disorder are ingrained in the person, active throughout the day and are never gone. They are considered to be part of their personality because this part of them seemed to be or was always present.

Those with this disorder would be considered in the field of Psychiatry to have a personality disorder. Those who have personality disorders may have no memory to contradict the Thought that caused them to have a problem. Therefore, they are considered to be people who behave in a particular way as part of their personality.

The psychiatric associations and books on psychiatry label personality disorders and other such disorders with such a huge number of labels and a contradicting number of symptoms that one could rightfully conclude that there should be a syndrome called Psychiatric Labeling Syndrome or Psychiatric Labeling Confusion Syndrome. But there is an underlying missing Thought in each of the types of Personality Disorders which can be identified.

Possible connected street name: Narcissistic Personality Disorder

Missing or inactive Thought: Missing or inactive Action Thought in the Task Thought of seeing one's self as having value or worth.
Injury: loss of the use of the concept in the Task Thought of one's self being of value or having worth
Reaction to injury: continual fight for acknowledgement of value from others
Thought group: Love

People with this disorder have a loss of the concept of being worthy or of value. It's not that they feel worthless. They don't feel anything as far as being of value and aren't aware of anything concerning this situation. The Action Thought is fighting to fix the feeling and fixing the feeling takes priority in every aspect of the person's life but the problem is that they are trying to fix the feeling by overpowering or controlling another person. Feeling as if one has value or worth is part of "The Natural State of Being" and when it is not there an emptiness is felt. After a while the person only knows to do for itself.

This deep feeling of having no value or worth has no opposing Thought unless it comes from another person. Admitting they are wrong tends to decrease their Thought of worth even more and is not tolerated. This loss of the concept of feeling of being of worth in the world or of value causes the person to feel empty inside. They are basically introverts.

Since they do not have a sense of worth their value has to come from the reinforcement of their worth from others. What they consider important is whether they have a hot girlfriend/boyfriend so others can see them (which is sort of a superficial artificial perfection), whether they win an argument, whether they have the nicest things. Their world is a façade with no foundation.

They have a crippling need for the admiration and the envy of others since they can't get their sense of worth from themselves. To do that they need to be the best at everything. Their need to believe they can't be imperfect makes admitting mistakes impossible. They seem to have a grandiose sense of self-importance as well as a fragile ego but the truth is that they have a fragile ego with a fake sense of self-importance.

They defend their fragile egos by overvaluing themselves at the expense of others by looking down at others and giving themselves latitude while blaming others. If things don't work it is the fault of another not them and any success is considered to be by their actions. Deceptive behavior is sometimes used to bring them up or bring another down.

They often deal with the emptiness by being arrogant and reacting with rage. They have a lack of empathy and are known to be a bully.

Relationships are superficial to them because they aren't really present and if a relationship ends the partner is replaced. This is because they were merely used for value replacement anyway. Being left is an insult and they will fight with a messy divorce; stalk the former partner, act vindictively by spending or hiding money. They will fight for children even if they don't want them and it is not in the best interest of the children. They will replace the lost partner as soon as possible and do so with one that they would see as a step up. They are deceitful, they lie and they can go into a rage at any moment.

For those with this disorder trying to find their value or worth is unconsciously the most important thing and it dominates their life. The second most important thing is probably revenge.

There are four ways a person would deal with this disorder.

1. Called grandiose this person fills what is missing by building himself/herself up using fantasies or actual earned boosts while at the same time stepping on others but only if necessary.

2. Called malignant this person will purposely take from another as the main way of getting what they unconsciously feel will help them.

3. Called covert this person will try to fill their missing concept of value by believing they are great but others don't see it. To them all things would be the fault of the other person not them. A person with this type of disorder may go into a depression because the world never got their believed greatness. They feel they are a victim and blame the world.

4. Called communal this person feels they can replace their value by trying to save the world and they need to talk about it for reinforcement.

Possible connected street name: Borderline Personality Disorder

Missing or inactive Thought: Missing or inactive Action Thought in the Task Thought of having skills to care for one's self that would be in "The Natural State of Being".
Injury: loss of the use of the concept in the Task Thought of having skills to care for one's self.
Reaction to injury: desperate need to rely on others
Thought group: Love

The symptoms are:

1. Real or perceived belief that they cannot take care of themselves.
2. Instability and impulsivity, moody behavior
3. Obsessive fear of abandonment
4. less sense of self
5. belief that if they take a chance, they will die
6. may want to change their name etc.
7. angry to sad to cheerful in same hour, emotional instability.
8. daily moods.
9. always prepare for abandonment.
10. unstable interpersonal relationships
11. doesn't know who they are
12. change appearance often,
13. impulsivity with binges
14. often in financial trouble,
15. dangerous suicidal thoughts or attempts to avoid abandonment
16. cutting or hanging as a cry for help,
17. moods all over the place in short time
18. chronically feels empty or nothing inside
19. panic, angered by slight things
20. others in their life feel they walk on eggshells
21. very thin skinned and over feel
22. after anger they are remorseful and terrified then mad at self
23. within an hour can be set off by nothing of importance

24.   under stress may have paranoid thoughts
25.   acts like a child,

The unstable distorted self-image in this disorder would cause a chronic feeling of inadequacy and emptiness. This inadequacy would cause a need to lean on others for their very survival. Because of the extreme need for help of others there is a fear of real or imagined abandonment and a tendency toward unstable relationships.

Because they are unstable in how they see themselves they will consider themselves and others as good or bad in the extreme. When they evaluate someone, they do so in the context of needing them and if they do something that they consider to be unsupportive of how they think they will quickly change their opinion from idolization to devaluation. This concept of going from good to bad would also be in their concept of themselves and lead them to sabotage their own success.

This unstable need would cause impulsive and risky behavior like gambling, shoplifting, unsafe sex or drugs or alcohol, self-harm and suicide, intense mood swings, explosive anger, paranoia, dissociation, mood swings sometimes hourly, binge eating, self-harming, cutting, suicide or threats. These behaviors can be for the purpose of manipulating another person or for escape when all manipulation fails.

This disorder is directed toward the self and protecting the self in what is mostly the physical world.

Possible connected street name: Paranoid Personality Disorder

Missing or inactive Thought: Missing or inactive Action Thought in the Task Thought of trust in one's self or others or the world that would be from "The Natural State of Being".
Injury: loss of the use of the Concept Thought in the Task Thought toward trust in one's self or others or the world that would be from "The Natural State of Being".
Reaction to injury: fear and mistrust in all general situations
Thought group: Truth

In this person there is a pervasive pattern of suspiciousness and hypersensitivity. They suspect others are harming them or deceiving them. They are preoccupied with loyalty of friends and test that loyalty. If something better comes along, they won't be loyal so they feel others won't be loyal as well. They have an obsession with loyalty of those attached to self. Because there is no active contradicting Thought they don't know they have this disorder. They have low insight because in most cases they wouldn't trust what is said anyway. They are reluctant to confide in others because others will not be trustworthy. They read meanings into things. They are unforgiving and hold grudges. They will be vengeful and consider things disrespectful. I have to be at the best table or its disrespect. They are insulted if not at highest level and angry with others at table one, because being at table two is attacking their character or reputation. They will counterattack. "You put me at rubies and I need to be at diamonds". They will minimize praise because their framework will collapse.

The unusual thing about this disorder is that there is a belief that others have a hidden agenda. It does not take much to believe this especially if there were incidents in their lives where someone's dishonesty supported their beliefs. They believe others are out to get them. They doubt loyalty of others. They are hypersensitive to criticism, have trouble working with others, are quick to anger and hostile, are detached from society and isolated, have trouble seeing their own problems, are argumentative, are jealous and defensive, are sensitive to setbacks, have trouble relaxing, distrust authority, are confrontational, hostile, critical, controlling, resentful, sensitive, jealous, suspicious.

All of the symptoms come along with living in a world where they do not trust themselves and the things they would do and therefore don't trust others. It is a sad place to be. They need to take chances to trust others and if the others fail, they need to understand the humanity of that person and try again and again.

Possible connected street name: Antisocial Personality Disorder

Missing or inactive Thought: Missing or inactive Action Thought in the Task Thought of caring about others in general as planned in "The Natural State of Being".
Injury: loss of the use of the Concept Thought in the Task Thought toward caring about others.
Reaction to injury: no distinction of right and wrong concerning people. Needs of the self are everything.
Thought group: Love

A person with this disorder cannot put themselves in the shoes of another and most importantly doesn't care to.

The following words describe people with this disorder: dishonest, manipulative, law breaking, risk taking, no remorse, irresponsible, subtle abuse, unhealthy relationships, hostility and aggressions, impulsive, disregard for right or wrong, lying and disruptive, exploiting others, callous and cynical, disrespectful to others, uses charm and wit to manipulate others, arrogant superiority and opinionated, criminal behavior, violates rights of others through intimidation and dishonesty, fails to plan ahead, lack of empathy or remorse toward others, fails to learn from negative behavior, irresponsible in work and finances (before age 15) aggression toward people and animals, theft, destruction of property, deceitfulness, rule breaking, no impulse control.

The self in this situation is intact but there is no care about others and never was. A good example is of the young woman who shot her parents and when in the interrogation room said, "What's going to happen to me?"

Possible connected street name: Dependent Personality Disorder

Missing or inactive Thought: Missing or inactive Action Thought in the Task Thought toward the thought in "The Natural State of Being" to reach a basic truth.
Injury: loss of the use of the concept in the Task Thought of confidence of their own ability to come to accurate conclusions.
Reaction to injury: floundering, need for help in everyday decision making
Thought group: Truth

This person has a lack of self confidence in their judgement and abilities to reach a basic truth. This causes the person to feel helpless, fearful and have an excessive pervasive need to be taken care of. There is difficulty not so much in making everyday decisions but in believing in their decisions without advice and reassurance from others. This leads them to be uncomfortable when alone since being alone would mean they were with someone in whom they had no confidence in decision making.

This lack of confidence causes fear of expressing disagreement because they just are not sure. If a relationship ends, they will seek the next relationship immediately to avoid having to take care of themselves.

Their self esteem is also damaged and they will volunteer to do whatever is unpleasant to get support from others.

This person is not aggressive and feels generally lower than others.

Possible connected street name: Histrionic Personality Disorder

Missing or inactive Thought: Missing or inactive Action Thought in the Task Thought toward seeing one's self as having value or worth placed as it would be in "The Natural State of Being".
Injury: loss of the use of the concept in the Task Thought of one's self being of value or having worth.
Reaction to injury: continual fight for acknowledgement of value using means that reflect their tendency to be an extrovert.
Thought group: Truth

These people are basically extroverts who have the same disorder as narcissistic personality disorder but are outgoing instead of introverted. They are not looking for love to show their worth but for their worth to be factually true.

The symptoms of this disorder are constant attention seeking, over dramatization, being uncomfortable when not the center of attention, being sexually seductive or provocative, rapid shifting and shallow expression of emotions, constant use of physical actions to draw attention to self, speech style is excessively impressionistic and lacking detail, self-dramatization, having theatrically and exaggerated expression of emotion, being suggestible, considering relationships to be more than they are.

People with this disorder have a loss of the concept of being worthy or of value. It's not that they feel worthless but they believe that it is a fact that they are worthless and their views are worthless. The Action Thought is not fighting to feel worthy but the person wants to feel worthy and on equal ground to others. They are not out to impress so others feel they are of value but so they feel they themselves are of value.

Since they do not have a sense of worth their value has to come from the reinforcement of their worth from others but not for them to gain approval of others but that they can gain approval for themselves. What they consider important is not whether they have a hot girlfriend or boyfriend but that they *are* the hot girlfriend or boyfriend.

It is not the same missing self-worth as narcissism because the goal is not approval by others but approval by themselves.

Possible connected street name: Avoidant Personality Disorder

Missing or inactive Thought: Missing or inactive Action Thought in the Task Thought toward seeing one's self as pleasing and equal to others
Injury: loss of the use of the concept in the Task Thought of being pleasing and equal to others
Reaction to injury: to avoid any situation where they have to deal with their negative Thoughts and do so with fear.
Thought group: Truth

Since the opposite of pleasing is repellant, one could understand why a person who thought this of themselves would want to avoid the people they believe think this of them which would be everyone except family. Since they live in the world of people, they would be facing this Concept constantly. In addition, they would continually examine themselves with no sense of equality or self forgiveness for being human.

The symptoms of this disorder are constant apprehension, concern about trivial matters, being overwhelmed by the thought of a meeting in coming days, feel unwelcome all the time, self-isolation for long periods of time, low self-esteem, having hard time seeing ones accomplishments, reluctant to meet new people, preoccupied with abandonment, reluctant to pursue intimacy due to fear, substance abuse, reluctant to take life risks, sensitive to criticism, emotional and easily upset, avoid occupational activities, unwilling to get involved with people, show resistance within intimate relationships, preoccupied with being criticized, inhibited in new interpersonal situations, sees self as socially inept, reluctant to take personal risks for fear of embarrassment.

These are called disorders because there is a possibility that the cause is from influence in the world though their origin is not definitely known. It may be that the Thoughts from "The Natural State of Being" were not placed before the child was born as they should have been or it may be that a situation caused these Thoughts that would have been placed from "The Natural State of Being" to be stopped or lay dormant. Either way this happened before memory was formed which is known because for the person there is no contrary Thought.

They are called personality disorders because they are pervasive meaning they are there in every aspect of the persons daily life.

This book is a work in progress. I gave you the basics and some examples of illnesses. More research needs to be done.

CHAPTER 16
Just a list of Thoughts

Each Thought that is planted in the being has a different purpose. Each Thought also has a different importance. Some Thoughts simply teach how to complete an educational task which if the Thought is missing would give the person the inability to do a school task like creative writing or math. Some Thoughts are life changing which if missing the loss would leave the person completely disabled.

This chapter and the following list is for the purpose of giving you an idea of some of the Thoughts that are planted in the being for it to be a human being. This chapter is also for you to get an idea of how intricate and ingenious this preplanned Thought system is.

You don't have to read them all but it really is interesting. This is by far a partial list. The asterisks show Thoughts in syndromes, disorders or behaviors.

General Foundational Thoughts
These Thoughts are foundational Thoughts of Love, Life and Truth. As you can see from this list each foundational Thought has the ability to be expressed or received.

LOVE
Thought to express Love of Self.
Thought to express Love for Others.
Thought to express Love beyond the self such as toward mankind or God.
Thought to receive Love of the self from others: (socialization).
Thought to receive Love from mankind or God.
Thought to receive Love from the self.

LIFE
Thought to express Life.
Thought to receive Life.

TRUTH
Thought to express Truth.
Thought to receive Truth.
Thought to receive Truth from mankind or God.

The rest of this list of Thoughts is to show you the kind of Thoughts that were placed in the Mind.

GENERAL PLANTED THOUGHTS FOR ENJOYMENT AND PROSPERITY

Thought that there is a physical self (body).
Thoughts of Personal talents.
Thoughts of Personal characteristics.
Thought of love of self as its gender.
The Thought of self as a human.
Thought of placement of the self in the world.
Thought of self as a whole.
Thought of happiness.
Thought of the desire to make another happy.
Thought of worthiness of the self.
Thought of peace.
Thought of hope.
Thought of the self being visible to others.
Thought to express own feelings.
Thoughts of Child to Adult Thought Series.
Thoughts of Reproduction/Sexuality.

GENERAL PLANTED THOUGHTS FOR GROWTH THROUGH LEARNING

Thought of Memory. -
Thought of Assimilation.
Thought of planted physical reflex thoughts.
Thought of seeing and hearing.
Thought of reflex actions deactivating and voluntary actions activating.
Thought of mentally representing an object that is not present with physically concrete Thoughts.
Thought of deactivating mentally representing an object that is not present with physically concrete Thoughts.
Thought of mentally representing an object that is not present with logical Thoughts.
Thought of making sounds.
Thought to use the body.
Thought of words as symbols.
Thought to purposely make sounds.
Thought of reaching to touch.
Thought of sounds connected to objects.
Thought of self as an image.
Thought to visually change what is associated with audition.
Thought of coordination of systems.
Thought of looking at sound source.
Thought of intent.
Thought of self separate from world.

Thought of equilibrium.
Thought to Accommodate.
Thought that a face is of some significance.
Thought of self recognition.
Thought of representational play.
Thought concerning the speed of Thought.
Thought of differed imitation.
Thought to use the body to accomplish a goal.
Thought to receive satisfaction from its actions.
Thought to seek satisfaction in its actions.
Thought to repeat seeking satisfaction from its actions.
Thought that objects and sounds are connected as a unit. -
Thoughts of sounds having a purpose.
Thought of being able to do what others do (imitating). -
Thought of continuity of self.
Thought of the visual face connected to feelings of what adults would call being loved.
Thought that a particular image connects with the concept of nourishment and/or love.
Thought of a sound unconsciously connecting to Thoughts of satisfaction or displeasure.
Thought of putting actions together toward a goal.
Thought of producing purposeful sounds.
Thought of objects being used with other objects.
Thought of confidence that truth is to be believed.
Thought of curiosity about objects.
Thought to use words.
Thought of gaining the attention of others through actions.
Thought to convey something by making gestures of yes or no.
Thought of being separate from the people and objects around them.
Thought of their actions being able to cause things to happen.
Thought that objects have a purpose of function.
Thought to have a mental representation of objects.
Thought of relating to other children.
The Thought of imagining.
Thought of sorting.
Thought of playing.
Thoughts of confidence/desire to do more things.
Thought that other children will be fun.
Thought of purposeful concern and affection for others without prompting.
Thought to share.
Thought to create stories or play.
Thought of matching.
Thought to show feelings.
Thought to see things from another person's point of view.
Thought to count.
Thought to copy.
Thought to link numbers to objects.
Thought of understanding time and waiting.

Thought of opposites.:
Thought to predict what's next.
Thought of having imaginary friends.
Thought of expressing likes and dislikes.
Thought to seek new experiences.
Thought to recall stories.
Thought to pretend.
Thought to bring others into their world.
Thought of being a particular gender.
Thought of conservation of numbers.
Thought to tell a story.
Thought to want to please friends.
Thought of knowing the difference between real and fantasy.
Thought to use future tense.
Thought to use word I.
Thought of having a physical self apart from its environment and others.
Thought to place words heard and things seen in memory as symbols or concepts for real objects.
Thought to pretend one object to be another.
Thought to use the make-believe world.
Thought to carry out concrete things.
Thought to play for an outcome or reach a result.
Thought of games rules center around rules and regulations.
Thought that symbols are tools.
Thought of being able to anticipate consequences.
Thought that objects or sets of objects stay the same even when they are changed or made to look different.
Thought that the amount of liquid in a short, wide cup is equal to that in a tall, skinny glass, for example (weight conservation).
Thought to move from what is concrete.
Thought to apply logic to physical things or objects.
Thought to recognize relationships among various things in serial order.
Thought to sort objects according to different criteria.
Thought to classify objects according to several features and order them in series along a single dimension or feature such as size, shape.
Thought to consider more than one feature of a problem at a time.
Thought to think backwards.
Thought to view things from another person's perspective even if the viewer is wrong.
Thought quantity and size can be separate.
Thought to put things in order of importance or prioritize.
Thought of how others may feel.
Thought to follow up on ideas.
Thought that something can be nonmaterial or an idea, feeling or quality.
Thought of reasoning about hypothetical problems.
Thought to reason consciously making sense of things, applying logic, and adapting or justifying practices, institutions, and beliefs based on new or existing information.

Thoughts about moral, philosophical, ethical, social, and political issues that require theoretical and abstract reasoning.

Thought to begin to use deductive logic, or reasoning from a general principle to specific information.

Thought of concern for the future.

Thought to form ideas/hypotheses based on best available evidence with trial and error.

Thought of reflecting on a thought.

Thought to systematically plan for the future and reason about hypothetical situations.

Thought to put the right actions together.

Thought that their actions have a relationship to each other.

Thought of things becoming representative of standing for other things.

Thought to link symbols/signs and reality.

Thought that things have a commonality.

Thought to consider three factors at a time.

Thought of subsets.

Thought to reflect on own thinking.

Some Later Activated Thoughts

Activated Thought: The world is made using certain rules or laws.

Activated Thought: The rules both physical or mental things learned are true.

Activated Thought: There is a drive to learn the rules

Activated Thought: Input of the senses with no learned solidity in two dimensions

Activated Thought: Sensory input connects to relief from disequilibrium.

Activated Thought: to assimilate.

Activated Thought: to put schema or new Thoughts in memory.

Activated Thought: objects do not disappear (object permanence). *The rule that objects are physically solid as well as 3 dimensional presents itself.*

Activated Thought: objects are physically solid and cannot go through each other is believed

Activated Thought: prior sensory input may not be true. The Thought that images as just pictures, sounds as just sounds etc. does not represent what is true.

Activated Thought: objects are three dimensional and real is believed.

Activated Thought: to accommodate.

Activated Thought: real physical objects work together with other real physical objects. *This*

Activated Thought: that the concepts in the Mind can represent something other than what they were previously presented to be. *This brings into play the concept of symbols as words and symbols as other objects allowing the child to play with toys. This allows the child to see the larger picture by looking at the smaller as we would look at a map to understand geography.*

Prior to any of these new Thoughts being activated the belief in the child was that each thing was exactly what it was thought or objectively presented to be. A sound was just a sound, a vision was just a vision, an object though now permanent was simply an object.

Activated Thought: an imagined concept can be used for a purpose other than what was previously thought.

Activated Thought: one concept is linked to another (continuity)

Activated Thought: to make a whole Concept out of coherent and connected smaller Concepts.

Activated Thought: I am separate from the environment

Activated Thought: the environment is separate from me.

Activated Thought: things are alive (early stage) because they move by themselves.

Activated Thought: inanimate things are not alive because they don't move by themselves.

Activated Thought: the concept to distinguish what is real from what is not real.

Activated Thought: I can connect an action to an object or action falsely for the purpose of learning. (this later becomes lying).

Activated Thought: Thought to deactivate the Thought of pretending for the purpose of learning.

Activated Thought: what is imagined or believed may not be true.

Activated Thought: The Thought to deactivate the Thought of pretending (object representation with belief) for the sake of learning.

Activated Thought: what is true is activated.

Post birth Thoughts of behavior in opposition to "The Natural State of Being".

Blame
Lying
Judging others
Pride
Denial
Selfishness
Wrong priorities
Resentment
Arrogance
Betrayal
Fear of loss of life security
Attention seeking
Truth avoidance
Validation
Price to do right too high:
Dominance
Revenge
False hope
Lack of fairness
Rage
Confusion
No accepted values
No self admiration
Antagonism
Insensitivity
Low empathy
Immorality
Dependence
Cowardliness
False beliefs
Negativity

Obsession
Avoidance of responsibility
Pathological lying
Impulsiveness
Lack of long-term goals
Excitement seeking
Overstepping bounds
Worthlessness
Lack of trust
Lack of concept of self
Self-worth imbalance
Underlying inadequacy
Underlying inadequacy with no forgiveness
Crippling need for admiration
Projection
Above others
Superficiality
Self is perfect
Above others
No moral self awareness
Anger
Negative beliefs
Just didn't dawn
Lack of self value
Shame
Awareness of weakness
Money/power driven
God complex
No imagination
No logic
Lack of a world view
Comparing
Irresponsible
Afraid of success
Risk taking
Hostility
Callousness
Don't know self
Privilege
Mistrust
Gangs
I'm great you're garbage
Bulling
threatening
intimidating
stealing

hostility
lack of self respect
lack of respect for others
unrealizing things that are incidental
Confusion
Pretentiousness
Shyness
Entitlement
Blame
Greed
envy
immorality
idolatry
strife
jealousy
dishonesty
Getting worth from another
guilt
belief of being valueless
Betrayal
Unwillingness to pay the price of morality
Lack of self-acceptance
Ignorance

CHAPTER 17
Heal Yourself

The syndromes and disorders discussed here are only a few of the illnesses that are caused when something goes wrong with the placement or activation of a Thought. For every Thought placed in the person there is a situation that could go wrong. I worked out the main ones but you have to work out the ones that I have not covered that you may come across yourself.

People in the psychiatric field analyze their patients by examining things that happened in their childhoods and typically placing blame on a parent. They listen to their stories and compare their behaviors. Then they label them and sometimes actually are able to heal them unless they have a Prebirth Syndrome or a missing Thought disorder.

If they can, they give them ideas and information to help them cope. Very few are healed. I know of only two who were healed who had a syndrome. One took eleven years and the other took being sentenced to life in prison.

Now that you know the secret to why the syndromes and disorders happened, the healing can begin as the patient realizes the origin and the cause of their disorder and unusual behavior and can work on replacing the missing Thoughts.

What needs to be done to heal is the same as learning. When you learn you have a Thought. You realize the Thought is incorrect. You replace the Thought with another. With these syndromes you need to work on finding out what the Thought you have that is in opposition to "The Natural State of Being". Once you do you have to apply what is true from "The Natural State of Being" or you could say what is actually true.

Often only the person can figure out what the missing Thought is because people are so complex and it's their Thought. I spoke to a serial killer who did this, learned about a woman with multiple personality disorder who did this and others. It is possible and it is doable. You can heal. You just need to put in the work.

Just for fun: Astore Syndrome

Astore Syndrome is called homosexuality in the psychiatric world. Those who have it can be unaffected in every other aspect of their lives or their lives can revolve around it or revolve around trying to get away from it.

Some will marry and have children but when the syndrome takes over it dominates even if it means a loss of family. This is because the fulfillment of the Thought that is missing precedes the rest of the Thoughts in the series and it has to be fulfilled first. If the other Thoughts in the series are still intact, they will be secondary to Astore Syndrome but will still need to be fulfilled.

Therefore, the person can have a loving relationship with the opposite sex without any difficulty or possibly with just the difficulty of not being sexually attracted because the prior stage was not fulfilled or be sexually attracted to both those of the opposite sex and those of the same sex.

A very popular musician who didn't know he had Astore Syndrome or know of its existence wrote a song about his experience. I don't have permission to use it nor have I asked for it so if you want this understanding, you will have to figure out who it is on your own. I also haven't included the name of the song but it can probably be figured out by the explanation.

The song does a great job of taking the person through the life of someone with Astore Syndrome. It is not necessary that you read this but if you are interested, read it and figure out who wrote the song and what the song is then read it again with the song and lyrics for better understanding. The explanation is in italics in case you are interested.

I have to give you some backstory on him. He was in love for most of his life with a woman who he said was the love of his life and who he called his common-law wife. When he died, he left a small but equal amount of money to his coworkers and to the man with whom he had a long-term sexual relationship. The remainder of the money, which was substantial, and his house was left to the woman he repeatedly stated that he loved.

Astore Syndrome took up a chunk of his life and left a chunk untouched as well. He often bounced from one feeling to another with bouts of confusion in between. I have to say I really liked this man. This I believe to be the explanation of his song. Figure it out if you want to.

> *In Line 1&2: He is asking if what he feels for the woman that he loves is real or the feelings caused by the actions to relieve Astore Syndrome are real. Which is real and which is fantasy.*
> *In line 3&4: He realizes he is caught in a downward spiral with no escape.*
>
> *In line 5&6: He looks to heaven for answer.*
> *In lines 7–9: He humbly indicates he is no one and his life is simply ups and downs and he is not asking for sympathy since he had a good life but he still wants help.*
> *In Line10-11: He gives up and states he doesn't care I assume to God.*
> *Lines 12-16: He talks about killing a man, how it ended his life and how sorry he was to his mother. I didn't like this song at first because it struck me as annoying*

that a man who shot a man in his head would be feeling sorry for himself. But then when I understood Astore Syndrome I realized that the man he killed was him when he acted on the drive from Astore Syndrome and that since he shot himself in the head in the song that action would have insured that he basically died.

<u>In lines 17&18:</u> He apologizes to his mother who he seems to love very much.
<u>In line 19:</u> He has hope again that he will return.
<u>In line 20:</u> He gives up again and basically says never mind just carry on it doesn't matter anyway. This bounce from despair to hope happens over and over again.

<u>In lines 21-25:</u> Astore Syndrome hits again and he acts upon it. His reaction sends shivers down his spine and he says goodbye because he has to face the truth which he thinks is that what he doesn't want will always win and the opposing part of him where the love of his life lives is dead.

<u>In lines 26:</u> He says he doesn't want this but it's okay. But in the next breath it is seen as death to him and he doesn't want to die.
<u>In line 27:</u> He says he sometimes wished he had never been born. This man liked himself very much and he liked his music. When Astore Syndrome hit him, he wished he was never born but the other parts of the day he was a happy man. This is why he used the term sometimes.

<u>In line 28:</u> He shows that the actions from Astore Syndrome make him feel like he is just a silhouette of a man.
<u>In lines 29-34:</u> This part is what throws everyone off. That is because the words are bound together to say one thing...I am confused. He reflects on his life which is a bouncing storm of confusion.
<u>In lines 35-37:</u> He says he is nobody so why not let him go which is intwined with pleading to spare his life from this monstrosity (Astore Syndrome drive),

<u>In Line 38-45:</u> He is pleading to be let go and a verbal fight ensues by the forces that say he will never be let go.
<u>In Line 46:</u> He talks about the devil having him

<u>In lines 47-49:</u> He is angry
<u>In line 50:</u> He just wants to get away from it

<u>In lines 51 to end:</u> He gives up again.

I am sure this artist didn't know himself what he was saying. Explaining the syndromes is hard and I am very grateful to this man for his words. I only wish I had this information to have given him when he could have used it. I have no doubt understanding would have brought him happiness and relief.